POLITICAL ECONOMY

AND THE

UNITIVE PRINCIPLE

T.Collins Logan

Citations for all quotations from sources not already in the public domain are provided with each quote.

Cover photo & design by T.Collins Logan.

First Edition, May 5, 2013
ISBN 0-9770336-5-1

Published by the Integral Lifework Center
PO Box 221082
San Diego, CA 92192
www.integrallifework.com

For Future Generations

OTHER BOOKS BY T.COLLINS LOGAN

Being Well: Beginning the Journey of Integral Lifework

Memory: Self

True Love: Integral Lifework Theory & Practice

Essential Mysticism

The Vital Mystic: A Guide to Emotional Strength & Spiritual Enrichment

A Progressive's Guide to the New Testament

Please also visit www.integrallifework.com and www.tcollinslogan.com for articles, updates, discussion and additional information about the work of T.Collins Logan.

Special Thanks

Special thanks to the creators and contributors at *Beams and Struts* (www.beamsandstruts.com) for inspiring me to complete this effort; without the catalyzing discussion there, I may have let these ideas languish on the back burner for another decade or two. In particular, thanks to Trevor M. for inviting my participation and providing both encouragement and some superb resources, and to Joe C., Kaine D., Benjamin L., David L., David M., and Lincoln M. for their own resources, questions and observations. Thanks also to the brave souls who waded through early drafts of this book and provided feedback, and to Valerie H. for offering helpful insights on community development. And of course much gratitude to my wife Mollie, who consistently creates an oasis in the desert for me.

TABLE OF CONTENTS

Getting a Handle on Property

"When I was told to believe everything, I could believe nothing, and I knew not where to stop. I consulted the philosophers, I searched their books and examined their various theories; I found them all alike proud, assertive dogmatic, professing, even in their so-called skepticism, to know everything, proving nothing, scoffing at each other. This last trait, which was common to all of them, struck me as the only point in which they were right.....

We have no means of measuring this vast machine, we are unable to calculate its workings; we know neither its guiding principles nor its final purpose; we do not know ourselves, we know neither our nature nor the spirit that moves us; we scarcely know whether man is one or many; we are surrounded by impenetrable mysteries. These mysteries are beyond the region of sense, we think we can penetrate them by the light of reason, yet we fall back on our imagination. Through this imagined world each forces a way for himself which he holds to be right; none can tell whether his path will lead him to the goal. Yet we long to know and understand it all. The one thing we do not know is the limit of the knowable."

Rousseau, *Emile*, "The Creed of a Savoyard Vicar"

When I first began to theorize about the transformative practice of Integral Lifework, I was extrapolating a working hypothesis from observing what really seemed to help people. That is, my starting point was a specific array of benefits reported to me by my clients and students as the result of various self-nourishing practices - benefits which echoed or amplified my own experience, and from which I began to assemble a few distinct and recurring patterns of cause and effect. Then I attempted to discern and intuit some underlying principles that might organize and even govern those recurring patterns, with the hope of assembling an internally cohesive system of understanding and managing what was clearly a multifaceted and complex process. I was, essentially, working backwards from observed evidence to cohesive principles. This also involved researching and integrating perspectives from many different disciplines that had informed the initial practices themselves, including philosophy, psychology, education, spirituality and the alternative healing arts. The process demanded holding many ideas in a neutral space, then integrating them through meditation and disciplined habit. But something unexpected happened along the way, and that was the realization that, when I reversed the flow and began applying those principles in different situations, the scope of real world application expressed itself in flexible, seemingly fractal ways. The principles did not just apply to holistic self-care through a mainly interior lens - which was the central focus of my initial work - they also could be utilized to explore effective nourishment in ever-widening arenas of intention and action.

In the course of writing *True Love,* the first fruits of drawing together the many disparate input streams into the Integral Lifework frame, I was only just beginning to understand the implications of this flexible scope. I was in fact fairly tentative in my efforts to expand Integral Lifework into various arenas. For although it was clear that a multidimensional approach would be helpful in any situation, the manifestation of each dimension of nourishment across enlarging fields of activity felt at times daunting or even arrogant. So now, having had a few more years to mull things over, and with a few more empirical observations at hand, I hope to approach this topic with additional insight and confidence. At the same time, I am also acutely aware of the context in which I project my assertions. I am a product of my culture, upbringing, language, and life experiences. I am also operating with the constraints of a profoundly limited understanding of myself and my environment, and am subject, as always, to the pressures and events of current times and the phases, ebbs and flows of my biological existence. I am also not in a position to empirically test my hypotheses in any large-scale way. This aggregate awareness should, frankly, thwart me entirely from positing any menu of solutions to the challenges of our age, but I suspect such romantic attempts are my lot as a human being. Whenever I encounter a fragrant array of ideas during an afternoon walk, I can't help but want to share them with others. Likewise, when I discover something dangerous or alarming, I likewise wish to warn those I care about. So you will find both of those impulses expressed here.

Since political economy is such an expansive topic, we'll need some pretty hefty containers to sort it into digestible bits. In the past I have begun with an overview of Integral Lifework's twelve nourishment dimensions, then expanded out from there. But that doesn't work well for this exercise, and in fact I've been looking for ways to get a handle on political economy for a long time. Thankfully, I stumbled across an article by Carol M. Rose, "Romans, Roads, and Romantic Creators: Traditions of Public Property in the Information Age," that provided an *aha* moment about how to begin, and that is through a thoughtful categorization of property. Since that beginning, a cascade of insights and correlations have fit neatly into a *property matrix* that will hopefully allow us to organize property in a still more comprehensive way. So first we'll borrow a few terms from ancient Rome that were used in property law, mix in some layering concepts from Open Systems, add a property valuation strategy, then ferment this concoction within the multidimensional nourishment of Integral Lifework.

To begin, here are seven terms in Roman law that described different forms of property and ownership, which for the most part have endured in legal concepts in the U.S. and elsewhere:

- **Res nullius:** Something that could be owned, but as of yet is not. ***Potential property.***

- **Res privata:** Something that is privately owned. ***Private property.***

- **Res universitatis:** Property owned by an exclusive community for that community's benefit. ***Communal property.***

- **Res publica:** Property that could be owned (privatized) by anyone, but which is reserved for collective public use. Since this public benefit is usually enforced by the state, res publica is often associated with state oversight. ***Public domain property.***

- **Res communes:** Something tangible that cannot be exclusively owned by anyone, mainly because of its boundaryless nature. For example, the air, or the oceans. ***Common property.***

- **Res divini juris:** Something tangible that could be owned, but should not be owned because it is considered sacred. ***Sacred property.***

- **Ferae naturae:** ***Wild things.***

Apart from its *ownership* categorization, there is also a specific functional layer that different types of property inhabit. This is hinted at in a differentiation between tangible and intangible property, but this is an inadequate distinction. Instead, I'd like to apply something from my career in Information Technology: the Open Systems Interconnection (OSI) Model. In that model, all components of a network fit neatly into different layers, each having a unique and predictable function and scope (that is, the environment in which that function happens). Here is what these layers could represent as property designations:

- **Physical layer:** Tangible forms of property that are usually immovable and inert. For example: land, buildings.

- **Data Link layer:** Tangible forms of property that are usually immovable, and which often facilitate the conveyance of other tangible property. For example: roads, bridges, pipelines.

- **Network layer:** Tangible forms of property that are movable (even if temporarily immovable), and which may, by there nature, be able to contain and convey different layers of property. For example: vehicles, recording devices, communication and electrical lines, broadcast and relay antennas, computers, human beings, plants and animals, other living organisms.

- **Transport layer:** Property existing on the cusp between tangible and intangible, and which often acts as a conveyance medium for higher layer intangible property. For example: electricity, the electromagnetic spectrum, sound waves, psychoactive chemicals, the atmosphere.

- **Session layer:** Slightly more abstract intangible property that tends to be the nexus where all other layers intersect. For example: all creations of the mind, from fine art and inventions to philosophy and religion.

- **Presentation layer:** One more layer of abstraction and sophistication for intangible property, which tends to be intimately involved in creating lower property layers, and/or providing a context for the *application layer* to interact with those lower layers. For example: language, intelligence (human, animal or artificial), perception.

- **Application layer:** The most abstract and intangible forms of property, so far removed from the material world that their existence may be challenged and their contribution questioned, but which nevertheless seem both dependent on, and able to create, lower layers of property. For example: Ideas, feelings, memes...and perhaps karma, spirit and soul.

What is happening here? From one angle, we could say that this is simply a changing scope of property function. But from another, what we are really observing is the complexification and *abstraction* of property itself. This evolution appears to be one of the consequences of advancing human civilization and expanding consciousness, and there is a suggestion that as we have progressed through the industrial and information revolutions, the tendency has been for larger and larger swaths of property to function in the more abstract OSI layers. However, these layers are strictly and hierarchically dependent, for without the *physical layer* there could be no *network layer*, without the *network layer* there could be no *transport layer*, and so on. And dependences travel in the opposite direction as well, for the *application layer* leads to the ongoing creation of the *presentation layer*, and the *presentation layer* leads to the creation of the *session layer*. In many ways, this *abstraction* and complexification of property has made it increasingly challenging to assign property via the classic Roman *ownership* categories. That hasn't discouraged attempts to do so, via our legal system and emerging social mores, but a lot of cultural tension seems to be generated around the speed with which property within more abstract layers is being created and exchanged, regardless of the prevailing political economy.

And finally we require one more axis of the *property matrix*, and that is the *valuation* of property. Exchange value isn't really relevant here, mainly because the different approaches to political economy, and subjectively perceived levels of scarcity or abundance, will determine different exchange calculations. Part of what does matter to us here is use value, as calculated not just in practical utility (such as electricity) but also in the more theoretical sense of cultural capital. We might say that use value in this context is the aggregate of our active desire for something, the objective dependence on something even if it is not desired, and how something is socially esteemed within a given network, all included in a scatter plot across a given collective. However, all of these end up being somewhat interchangeable in terms of use value. For example, every household depends on water, but in one household water is greatly esteemed and conserved because of the cultural capital resulting from "being water conscious." Yet in another home water is highly desired, but not conserved at all, creating a similar use value via an alternate calculation. In still another household, where the family prefers to bathe in milk, drink only champagne and send out all their cloths to the cleaners, water may not be consciously esteemed or desired, but it is still in demand, a necessity one step removed, because the cows, grapes and professional washing machines all use water to produce the desired products and services. There will be countless instances where the perception of use value varies from one culture to the next, or even from one person to the next within a culture, with additional variability over time, so the aggregate of esteemed, desired and dependent utility begins to point us toward what may at least be a way to calculate an intersubjective use value.

However, this still isn't a sufficiently well-rounded method of valuation. I would like to add one more factor, and that is how skillfully property contributes to effective, balanced nourishment. What I mean by "effective, balanced nourishment" will become clear when we discuss the twelve nourishment centers later on, but what I am really trying to do here is add a vast, usually hidden repository of externalities to the calculation. For example, if water is polluted with toxins and carcinogens, then its use value is greatly reduced. This is not because someone who consumes the water knows anything about these toxins and carcinogens, it is instead a measurement of the additional costs required to offset these health dangers, either through treating people who get sick, treating the water so it becomes safe, or correcting the industrial practices that led to the pollution in the first place. When we combine such externalities with intersubjective use value calculations, we realize that any property that invites a widespread expectation of safe nourishment (such as water, food, air, etc.) has very high *holistic value.* So we see that quality supercedes quantity in such calculations; it does not matter if water is abundant, if that water is not safely consumable. In this way we redefine scarcity, because within *holistic value,* scarce quantity is equivalent to scarce (or difficult) quality.

There are of course instances in which we find an inverse relationship between "value" as defined in this way and either its perceived use value, or its actual exchange value in a given economy. This is what we might call *perverse utility.* An obvious example would be highly addictive, ultimately lethal drugs and drug delivery systems. If we used only one use factor, such as subjective desirability, we might arrive at a high perceived use value, and often a correspondingly high exchange value. But when we add effective and balanced nourishment to the equation, our new method of valuation quickly pushes something like cigarettes into the negative. At the opposite extreme, fast food with a low exchange value may nevertheless hold a high perceived use value, especially for people with little time to eat or a strong predilection for sugar, salt and fat. But if this food isn't nutritious, and in fact leads to many illnesses and premature death, then by any standard of effective, balanced nourishment this food ends up having a lower *holistic value.* Thus esteemed, desired and dependent utility must be balanced against property's contribution to nourishment, so that by understanding these complex relationships we can estimate a more practical valuation of all property. Exactly why a more well-rounded valuation is important will become obvious by the end of this book.

Taking these three axes together, we have the vertical axis of *ownership,* the horizontal axis of *abstraction,* and the depth axis of *holistic value.* With these we can plot the position of property in any context in a three-dimensional way. The evaluation of *property position* within this matrix has nifty utility in any discussion where politics, culture and economics intersect, so we'll be relying on it both to elaborate on existing institutions and systems, and to describe potential departures from the status quo. In our case, the notion of "property" will expand even into aspects of the political process itself; in fact we may need to stretch the metaphor to its limits. As for the concept of *personal* property, that will for the most part be excluded from this discussion, though its existence is both assumed and implied throughout as an inherent extension of personal freedom.

Diagram: Property Position

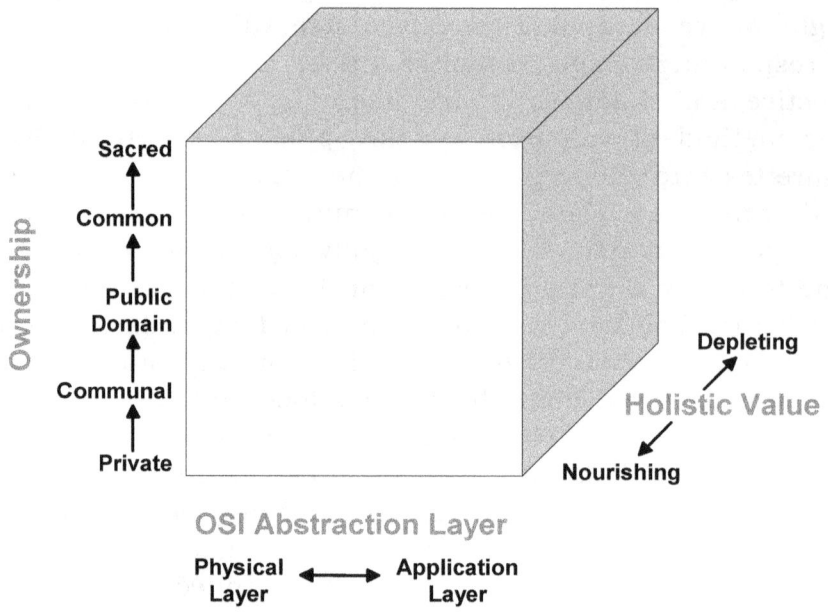

A Western Moral Lineage

One of the fundamental concerns of political economy is how to resolve the persisting tension between individual freedom and collective responsibility. The history of human civilization is, when viewed through this dynamic, a constant dance. At one end of the spectrum we find individual freedoms sacrificed for the collective good - that is, "good citizens" conforming to collective responsibilities in order to maximize collective benefits. At the other end of the spectrum we find individuals rejecting most or all collective responsibility in order to maximize personal freedom. And there are many gradations and variations in between. What is interesting is that differences in existential circumstances, values, and power relationships will completely change our assessment of outcomes here. If expectations of collective responsibility are felt to be too onerous or oppressive, then rebelling against them for the sake of personal freedom is cast as "liberation." If actions asserting individual freedom are destructive to social cohesion, infringe significantly upon the freedoms of others, or undermine collectively held benefits, they are often viewed as selfish or even sociopathic. This seems obvious but really these different perspectives are predicated on a complex substrate of moral valuations. So appreciating and categorizing that moral substrate is probably the most useful starting point in exploring economic, cultural and political systems and institutions.

Our guiding question for this examination is this: what are any of these systems and institutions attempting to accomplish? Or better yet, what do we want them to accomplish for ourselves, others and the world around us? What we want - that most basic of volitional queries - is central to our individual and collective moral orientation and development. And in a democratic society, where individual beliefs, hopes and aspirations are solicited to define - or at least substantially influence - the primary aims of society itself, that moral orientation and development is expressed through the election process. That is, at least, the intention of democracy. By wants and aspirations I of course mean *what we think is important.* What do we most value? What do we most cherish and honor and love? What is the dominant focus of our volition from moment-to-moment? This, in turn, informs all of our trust relationships, how we define exchanges and reciprocation, what we believe success or failure look like, what compassion and callousness look like to us, and which political ideologies resonate for us. For this examination, it also informs our tendencies in assessing what belongs in each of ancient Rome's seven categories of property, and how use value is calculated. We will see that, once we can clearly define moral development, we gain invaluable insight into how to balance personal freedoms with collective responsibility. In turn, we will identify what forms of political economy we can best tolerate, and which, hypothetically, would be most effective in embodying and reinforcing our values moving forward.

In one lineage of Western thought, there is a strong tradition of establishing the conditions, principles and processes of moral reasoning. Aristotle described morally virtuous character as "a mean between two vices: that which depends on excess and that which depends on defect; it is a mean because the vices respectively fall short of or exceed what is right in both passions and actions, while virtue both finds and chooses that which is intermediate." As an example, he clarifies, "For instance, both fear and confidence and appetite and anger and pity and in general pleasure and pain may be felt both too much and too little, and in both cases not well; but to feel them at the right times, with reference to the right objects, towards the right people, with the right motive, and in the right way, is what is both intermediate and best, and this is characteristic of virtue." Aristotle says this moral virtue is the result of how we have been "brought up in a particular way from our very youth," educated about which things ought to evoke pleasure, and which things ought to evoke pain, the navigation of which "is made perfect by habit." For Aristotle, all virtue is a rational activity that leads to flourishing (i.e. the soulful happiness that results from virtuous action), embodying qualities of courage, generosity, temperance, justice and moderation - all framed by one's interactions with others. At the heart of moral virtue is a simple principle: that virtuous love inspires a person to "act for his friend's sake, and sacrifice his own interest...even if no one is to know of it." Yet, for Aristotle, even this carefully reasoned explanation is subject to empirical observation, as he writes: "We must therefore survey what we have already said, bringing it to the test of the facts of life, and if it harmonizes with the facts we must accept it, but if it clashes with them we must suppose it to be mere theory." So Aristotelian moral virtue is a contemplative activity of moderating effect, reinforced or refuted by empirical observations, and refined through the loving interactions of friendship (see Aristotle's *Nicomachean Ethics* for the full discussion).

This basic framework for morality has been reconstituted and expanded upon over the years by various Western philosophical and religious thinkers, under the heading of

what academics call "normative ethics." Variations often
have to do with the source or justification for moral thought
and action, its outcomes, and sometimes a specific
spiritual, contemplative or empirical process required to
achieve a useful moral viewpoint, but the *qualities* of moral
thought and action remain surprisingly consistent with
Aristotle's "virtue ethics" offering, even using much of the
same language. So one perspective may hold such virtues
to be intrinsic, another that they are culturally inculcated,
another that they are divinely given, another that they
should be strictly derived from observed consequences, and
so on; but no matter the approach, the expressions of these
ethics look very much the same, with only subtle variations.
Again - for those who might take offense at such a sweeping
generalization - it is the culmination in specific qualities of
virtuous thought and action, and often the importance of
evaluating the outcomes of such actions, that has remained
relatively constant in this particular lineage.

This is, admittedly, not the standard academic organization
of moral philosophy, but I think we shall find it very useful.
So from Marcus Aurelius to David Hume, Plotinus to Jean
Jacques Rousseau, Saul of Tarsus to Immanuel Kant,
Aristotle to Adam Smith, or Grotius to Carol Gilligan, the
essential characteristics of moral intention and conduct
remain strikingly similar. They are nearly always expressed
as just, humble, kind, generous, judicious, self-controlled
relations that benefit of others without expectation of
reciprocation or reward, thus encouraging the flourishing of
everyone involved. To capture a small sampling of these
patterns, here are some relevant quotes:

> "Since the lawless man was seen to be unjust and the law-
> abiding man just, evidently all lawful acts are in a sense just acts; for
> the acts laid down by the legislative art are lawful, and each of these,
> we say, is just. Now the laws in their enactments on all subjects aim
> at the common advantage either of all or of the best or of those who
> hold power, or something of the sort; so that in one sense we call

those acts just that tend to produce and preserve happiness and its components for the political society.   And the law bids us do both the acts of a brave man (e.g. not to desert our post nor take to flight nor throw away our arms), and those of a temperate man (e.g. not to commit adultery nor to gratify one's lust), and those of a good-tempered man (e.g. not to strike another nor to speak evil), and similarly with regard to the other virtues and forms of wickedness, commanding some acts and forbidding others; and the rightly-framed law does this rightly, and the hastily conceived one less well. This form of justice, then, is complete virtue, but not absolutely, but in relation to our neighbor. And therefore justice is often thought to be the greatest of virtues, and 'neither evening nor morning star' is so wonderful; and proverbially 'in justice is every virtue comprehended'. And it is complete virtue in its fullest sense, because it is the actual exercise of complete virtue.   It is complete because he who possesses it can exercise his virtue not only in himself but towards his neighbor also; for many men can exercise virtue in their own affairs, but not in their relations to their neighbor. This is why the saying of Bias is thought to be true, that 'rule will show the man'; for a ruler is necessarily in relation to other men and a member of a society. For this same reason justice, alone of the virtues, is thought to be 'another's good', because it is related to our neighbor; for it does what is advantageous to another, either a ruler or a copartner.   Now the worst man is he who exercises his wickedness both towards himself and towards his friends, and the best man is not he who exercises his virtue towards himself but he who exercises it towards another; for this is a difficult task. Justice in this sense, then, is not part of virtue but virtue entire, nor is the contrary injustice a part of vice but vice entire. What the difference is between virtue and justice in this sense is plain from what we have said; they are the same but their essence is not the same; what, as a relation to one's neighbor, is justice is, as a certain kind of state without qualification, virtue.

....When the law speaks universally, then, and a case arises on it which is not covered by the universal statement, then it is right, where the legislator fails us and has erred by oversimplicity, to correct the omission - to say what the legislator himself would have said had he been present, and would have put into his law if he had known.   Hence the equitable is just, and better than one kind of justice - not better than absolute justice but better than the error that arises from the absoluteness of the statement. And this is the nature of the equitable, a correction of law where it is defective owing to its universality.   In fact this is the reason why all things are not determined by law, that about some things it is impossible to lay down a law, so that a decree is needed. For when the thing is indefinite the rule also is indefinite, like the leaden rule used in making the Lesbian molding; the rule adapts itself to the shape of the stone and is not rigid, and so too the decree is adapted to the facts. It is plain, then, what the equitable is, and that it is just and is better than one kind of justice.   It is evident also from this who the equitable man is; the man who chooses and does such acts, and is no stickler for his rights in a bad sense but tends to take less than his share though he has the law on his side, is equitable, and this state of character is equity, which is a sort of justice and not a different state of character."

Aristotle, *Nicomachean Ethics,* **350 B.C. (Trans. by W.D. Ross)**

"If I speak in the tongues of men and of angels, but don't have love, I am a noisy gong or a clanging cymbal. And if I have prophetic power, and understand all mysteries and all knowledge, and if I have sufficient faith to remove mountains, but don't have love, I am nothing. If I give away all I have to the poor, and deliver my body to be burned, but don't have love, it profits me nothing. Love is patient and kind, love does not envy or boast, it is not arrogant or rude. It does not insist on getting its own way, it is not irritable or resentful, it does not rejoice at wrongdoing, but rejoices in the truth. Love bears all things, believes all things, hopes all things, endures all things. Love never ends."

Apostle Paul, *First Letter to the Corinthians***, 1st Century A.D.**

"If you find in human life anything better than justice, truth, temperance, fortitude, and, in a word, anything better than you own mind's self-satisfaction in the things which it enable you to do according to right reason, and in the condition that is assigned to you without your own choice; if, say, you see anything better than this, turn to it with all your soul, and enjoy that which you have found to be the best. But if nothing appears to be better that the deity which is planted in you, which has subjected all your appetites to itself, and carefully examines all the impressions, and, as Socrates said, has detached itself from the persuasions of sense, and has submitted itself to the gods, and cares for mankind; if you find everything else smaller and of less value than this, give place to nothing else, for once you diverge and incline to it, you will no longer be able to, without distraction, give the preference to that good thing which is your proper possession and your own; for it is not right that anything of any other kind, such as praise from the many, or power, or enjoyment of pleasure, should come into competition with that which is rationally and politically good. All these things, even though they may seem to adapt themselves in a small degree, obtain the superiority all at once, and carry us away. I say simply and freely choose the better, and hold to it - though that which is useful is the better. Well, then, if it is useful to you as a rational being, keep to it; but if it is only useful to you as an animal, say so, and maintain your judgment without arrogance: only take care that you make the inquiry by a sure method."

Marcus Aurelius, *Thoughts of Marcus Aurelius Antoninus*, 2nd Century A.D. (Trans. by George Long)

"As it is not for those to speak of the graceful forms of the material world who have never seen them or known their grace - men born blind, let us suppose - in the same way those must be silent upon the beauty of noble conduct and of learning and all that order who have never cared for such things, nor may those tell of the splendor of virtue who have never known the face of Justice and of Moral-Wisdom beautiful beyond the beauty of Evening and of dawn. Such vision is for those only who see with the Soul's sight - and at the vision, they will rejoice, and awe will fall upon them and a trouble deeper than all the rest could ever stir, for now they are moving in the realm of Truth.

This is the spirit that Beauty must ever induce, wonderment and a delicious trouble, longing and love and a trembling that is all delight. For the unseen all this may be felt as for the seen; and this the Souls feel for it, every soul in some degree, but those the more deeply that are the more truly apt to this higher love - just as all take delight in the beauty of the body but all are not stung as sharply, and those only that feel the keener wound are known as Lovers. These Lovers, then, lovers of the beauty outside of sense, must be made to declare themselves.

What do you feel in presence of the grace you discern in actions, in manners, in sound morality, in all the works and fruits of virtue, in the beauty of souls? When you see that you yourselves are beautiful within, what do you feel? What is this Dionysiac exultation that thrills through your being, this straining upwards of all your Soul, this longing to break away from the body and live sunken within the veritable self? These are no other than the emotions of Souls under the spell of love.

But what is it that awakens all this passion? No shape, no color, no grandeur of mass: all is for a Soul, something whose beauty rests upon no color, for the moral wisdom the Soul enshrines and all the other hueless splendor of the virtues. It is that you find in yourself, or admire in another, loftiness of spirit; righteousness of life; disciplined purity; courage of the majestic face; gravity; modesty that goes fearless and tranquil and passionless; and, shining down upon all, the light of god-like Intellection."
Plotinus, *Enneads*, c. 270 A.D. (Trans. by Stephen MacKenna & B.S. Page)

"Where there is charity *[agape]* and wisdom there is neither fear nor ignorance. Where there is patience and humility there is neither anger nor worry. Where there is poverty and joy there is neither cupidity nor avarice. Where there is quiet and meditation there is neither solicitude nor dissipation. Where there is the fear of the Lord to guard the house the enemy cannot find a way to enter. Where there is mercy and discretion there is neither superfluity nor hard-heartedness."

Francis of Assisi, *Admonitions*, early 13th Century (Trans. by Paschal Robinson)

"Moral virtue may be considered either as perfect or as imperfect. An imperfect moral virtue, temperance for instance, or fortitude, is nothing but an inclination in us to do some kind of good deed, whether such inclination be in us by nature or by habituation. If we take the moral virtues in this way, they are not connected: since we find men who, by natural temperament or by being accustomed, are prompt in doing deeds of liberality, but are not prompt in doing deeds of chastity. But the perfect moral virtue is a habit that inclines us to do a good deed well; and if we take moral virtues in this way, we must say that they are connected, as nearly as all are agreed in saying. For this two reasons are given, corresponding to the different ways of assigning the distinction of the cardinal virtues. For, as we stated above, some distinguish them according to certain general properties of the virtues: for instance, by saying that discretion belongs to prudence, rectitude to justice, moderation to temperance, and strength of mind to fortitude, in whatever matter we consider these properties to be. In this way the reason for the connection is evident: for strength of mind is not commended as virtuous, if it be without moderation or rectitude or discretion: and so forth. This, too, is the reason assigned for the connection by Gregory, who says (Moral. xxii, 1) that "a virtue cannot be perfect" as a virtue, "if isolated from the others: for there can be no true prudence without temperance, justice and fortitude": and he continues to speak in like manner of the other virtues. Augustine also gives the same reason (De Trin. vi, 4). Others, however, differentiate these virtues in respect of their matters, and it is in this way that Aristotle assigns the reason for their connection (Ethic. vi, 13). Because, as stated above, no moral virtue can be without prudence; since it is proper to moral virtue to make a right choice, for it is an elective habit. Now right choice requires not only the inclination to a due end, which inclination is the direct outcome of moral virtue, but also correct choice of things conducive to the end, which choice is made by prudence, that counsels, judges, and commands in those things that are directed to the end. In like manner one cannot have prudence unless one has the moral virtues: since prudence is "right reason about things to be done," and the starting point of reason is the end of the thing to be done, to which end man is rightly disposed by moral virtue. Hence, just as we cannot have speculative science unless we have the understanding of the principles, so neither can we have prudence without the moral virtues: and from this it follows clearly that the moral virtues are connected with one another....

All the moral virtues are infused together with charity *[agape]*. The reason for this is that God operates no less perfectly in works of grace than in works of nature. Now, in the works of nature, we find that whenever a thing contains a principle of certain works, it has also whatever is necessary for their execution: thus animals are provided with organs whereby to perform the actions that their souls empower them to do. Now it is evident that charity *[agape]*, inasmuch as it directs man to his last end, is the principle of all the good works that are referable to his last end. Wherefore all the moral virtues must needs be infused together with charity *[agape]*, since it is through them that man performs each different kind of good work.

It is therefore clear that the infused moral virtues are connected, not only through prudence, but also on account of charity *[agape]*: and, again, that whoever loses charity *[agape]* through mortal sin, forfeits all the infused moral virtues....

Thomas Aquinas, *Summa Theologica* [Part 2, Q65-66], 1265-74,
(Trans. Fathers of the English Dominican Province)

"It is this kind of love which I should like us to have; at first it may not be perfect but the Lord will make it increasingly so. Let us begin with the methods of obtaining it. At first it may be mingled with emotion, but this, as a rule, will do no harm. It is sometimes good and necessary for us to show emotion in our love, and also to feel it, and to be distressed by some of our sisters' trials and weaknesses, however trivial they may be. For on one occasion as much distress may be caused by quite a small matter as would be caused on another by some great trial, and there are people whose nature it is to be very much cast down by small things. If you are not like this, do not neglect to have compassion on others; it may be that Our Lord wishes to spare us these sufferings and will give us sufferings of another kind which will seem heavy to us, though to the person already mentioned they may seem light. In these matters, then, we must not judge others by ourselves, nor think of ourselves as we have been at some time when, perhaps without any effort on our part, the Lord has made us stronger than they; let us think of what we were like at the times when we have been weakest.

Note the importance of this advice for those of us who would learn to sympathize with our neighbors' trials, however trivial these may be. It is especially important for such souls as have been described, for, desiring trials as they do, they make light of them all. They must therefore try hard to recall what they were like when they were weak, and reflect that, if they are no longer so, it is not due to themselves."

Teresa of Avila, *The Way of Perfection*, 1565-1566 (Trans. by E. Allison Peers)

"Man is, to be sure, an animal, but an animal of a superior kind, much farther removed from all other animals than the different kinds of animals are from one another; evidence on this point may be found in the many traits peculiar to the human species. But among the traits characteristic of man is an impelling desire for society, that is, for the social life-not of any and every sort, but peaceful, and organized according to the measure of his intelligence, with those who are of his own kind; this social trend the Stoics called 'sociableness.' Stated as a universal truth, therefore, the assertion that every animal is impelled by nature to seek only its own good cannot be conceded.

Some of the other animals, in fact, do in a way restrain the appetency for that which is good for themselves alone, to the advantage, now of their offspring, now of other animals of the same species. This aspect of their behavior has its origin, we believe, in some extrinsic intelligent principle, because with regard to other actions, which involve no more difficulty than those referred to, a like degree of intelligence is not manifest in them. The same thing must be said of children. In children, even before their training has begun, some disposition to do good to others appears, as Plutarch sagely observed; thus sympathy for others comes out spontaneously at that age. The mature man in fact has knowledge which prompts him to similar actions under similar conditions, together with an impelling desire for society, for the gratification of which he alone among animals possesses a special instrument, speech. He has also been endowed with the faculty of knowing and of acting in accordance with general principles. Whatever accords with that faculty is not common to all animals, but peculiar to the nature of man.

This maintenance of the social order, which we have roughly sketched, and which is consonant with human intelligence, is the source of law properly so called. To this sphere of law belong the abstaining from that which is another's, the restoration to another of anything of his which we may have, together with any gain which we may have received from it; the obligation to fulfill promises, the making good of a loss incurred through our fault, and the inflicting of penalties upon men according to their deserts.

From this signification of the word law there has flowed another and more extended meaning. Since over other animals man has the advantage of possessing not only a strong bent towards social life, of which we have spoken, but also a power of discrimination which enables him to decide what things are agreeable or harmful (as to both things present and things to come), and what can lead to either alternative: in such things it is meet for the nature of man, within the limitations of human intelligence, to follow the direction of a well-tempered judgment, being neither led astray by fear or the allurement of immediate pleasure, nor carried away by rash impulse. Whatever is clearly at variance with such judgment is understood to be contrary also to the law of nature, that is, to the nature of man."

Grotius, *De jure belli ac pacis*, 1625 (Trans. by Francis W. Kelsey)

"Men can desire, I say, nothing more excellent for the preservation of their being than that all should agree at every point that the minds and bodies of all should form, as it were, one mind and one body; that all should together endeavor as much as possible to preserve their being, and that all should together seek the common good of all. From this it follows that men who are governed by reason - that is to say, men who, under the guidance of reason, seek their own profit *[i.e. preservation of being]* - desire nothing for themselves which they do not desire for other men, and that, therefore, they are just, faithful and honorable."

Spinoza, *Ethics IV*, 1677 (Trans. by W.H. White)

"Thus he who acts well, not out of hope or fear, but by an inclination of his soul, is so far from not behaving justly that, on the contrary, he acts more justly than all others, imitating, in a certain way, as a man, divine justice. Whoever, indeed, does good out of love for God or of his neighbor, takes pleasure precisely in the action itself (such being the nature of love) and does not need any other incitement, or the command of a superior; for that man the saying that the law is not made for the just is valid. To such a degree is it repugnant to reason to say that only the law or constraint make a man just; although it must be conceded that those who have not reached this point of spiritual perfection are only susceptible of obligation by hope or by fear...."

Leibniz, *Opinion on the Principles of Pufendorf*, 1706 (Trans. by Patrick Riley, *The Political Writings of Leibniz*, Cambridge University Press, 1972)

"Now if life, without passion, must be altogether insipid and tiresome; let a man suppose that he has full power of modeling his own disposition, and let him deliberate what appetite or desire he would choose for the foundation of his happiness and enjoyment. Every affection, he would observe, when gratified by success, gives a satisfaction proportioned to its force and violence; but besides this advantage, common to all, the immediate feeling of benevolence and friendship, humanity and kindness, is sweet, smooth, tender, and agreeable, independent of all fortune and accidents. These virtues are besides attended with a pleasing consciousness or remembrance, and keep us in humor with ourselves as well as others; while we retain the agreeable reflection of having done our part towards mankind and society. And though all men show a jealousy of our success in the pursuits of avarice and ambition; yet are we almost sure of their good-will and good wishes, so long as we persevere in the paths of virtue, and employ ourselves in the execution of generous plans and purposes. What other passion is there where we shall find so many advantages united; an agreeable sentiment, a pleasing consciousness, a good reputation?"

Hume, *Enquiry Concerning the Principles of Morals,* **1751**

"As it is a divided sympathy which renders the whole set of passions just now mentioned, upon most occasions, so ungraceful and disagreeable; so there is another set opposite to these, which a redoubled sympathy renders almost always peculiarly agreeable and becoming. Generosity, humanity, kindness, compassion, mutual friendship and esteem, all the social and benevolent affections, when expressed in the countenance or behavior, even towards those who are not peculiarly connected with ourselves, please the indifferent spectator upon almost every occasion. His sympathy with the person who feels those passions, exactly coincides with his concern for the person who is the object of them. The interest, which, as a man, he is obliged to take in the happiness of this last, enlivens his fellow-feeling with the sentiments of the other, whose emotions are employed about the same object. We have always, therefore, the strongest disposition to sympathize with the benevolent affections....

The sentiment of love is, in itself, agreeable to the person who feels it. It sooths and composes the breast, seems to favor the vital motions, and to promote the healthful state of the human constitution; and it is rendered still more delightful by the consciousness of the gratitude and satisfaction which is must excite in him who is the object of it. Their mutual regard renders them happy in one another, and sympathy, with this mutual regard, makes them agreeable to every other person. With what pleasure we

look upon a family, through the whole of which reign mutual love
and esteem, where the parents and children are companions for one
another, without any other difference than what is made by
respectful affection on the one side, and kind indulgence on the
other; where freedom and fondness, mutual raillery and mutual
kindness, show that no opposition of interest divides the brothers,
nor any rivalship of favor sets the sisters at variance, and where
every thing presents us with the idea of peace, cheerfulness,
harmony and contentment?"

Adam Smith, *The Theory of Moral Sentiments,* **1759**

"My young friend, let us look within, let us set aside all personal
prejudices and see whither our inclinations lead us. Do we take more
pleasure in the sight of the sufferings of others or their joys? Is it
pleasanter to do a kind action or an unkind action, and which leaves
the more delightful memory behind it? Why do you enjoy the
theatre? Do you delight in the crimes you behold? Do you weep over
the punishment which overtakes the criminal? They say we are
indifferent to everything but self-interest; yet we find our
consolation in our sufferings in the charms of friendship and
humanity, and even in our pleasures we should be too lonely and
miserable if we had no one to share them with us. If there is no such
thing as morality in man's heart, what is the source of his rapturous
admiration of noble deeds, his passionate devotion to great merit
What connection is there between self-interest and this enthusiasm
for virtue? Why should I choose to be Cato dying by his own hand,
rather than Caesar in his triumphs? Take from our hearts this love of
what is noble and you rob us of the joy of life. The mean-spirited
man in whom these delicious feelings have been stifled among vile
passions, who by thinking of no one but himself comes at last to love
no one but himself, this man feels no raptures, his cold heart no
longer throbs with joy, and his eyes no longer fill with the sweet
tears of sympathy, he delights in nothing; the wretch has neither life
nor feeling, he is already dead.

There are many bad men in this world, but there are few of these
dead souls, alive only to self-interest, and insensible to all that is

right and good. We only delight in injustice so long as it is to our own advantage; in every other case we wish the innocent to be protected. If we see some act of violence or injustice in town or country, our hearts are at once stirred to their depths by an instinctive anger and wrath, which bids us go to the help of the oppressed; but we are restrained by a stronger duty, and the law deprives as of our right to protect the innocent. On the other hand, if some deed of mercy or generosity meets our eye, what reverence and love does it inspire! Do we not say to ourselves, "I should like to have done that myself"? What does it matter to us that two thousand years ago a man was just or unjust? And yet we take the same interest in ancient history as if it happened yesterday. What are the crimes of Cataline to me? I shall not be his victim. Why then have I the same horror of his crimes as if he were living now? We do not hate the wicked merely because of the harm they do to ourselves, but because they are wicked. Not only do we wish to be happy ourselves, we wish others to be happy too, and if this happiness does not interfere with our own happiness, it increases it. In conclusion, whether we will or not, we pity the unfortunate; when we see their suffering we suffer too. Even the most depraved are not wholly without this instinct, and it often leads them to self-contradiction. The highwayman who robs the traveler, clothes the nakedness of the poor; the fiercest murderer supports a fainting man."

Rousseau, *Emile*, "The Creed of a Savoyard Vicar," 1762 (Trans. by W. Conyngham Mallory)

"A certain tenderheartedness that is easily led into a warm feeling of sympathy is beautiful and lovable, for it indicates kindly participation in the fate of other people, to which the principles of virtue likewise lead. But this kindly passion is nevertheless weak and is always blind....If, by contrast, general affection towards humankind has become your principle, to which you always subject your actions, then your love towards the one in need remains, but it is now, from a higher standpoint, placed in its proper relationship to your duty as a whole. The universal affection is ground for participating in his ill-fortune, but at the same time it is also a ground of justice, in accordance with whose precept you must now forbear this action. Now as soon as this feeling is raised to its proper universality, it is sublime, but also colder....

The second sort of kindly feeling which is to be sure beautiful and lovable but still not the foundation of a genuine virtue is complaisance: an inclination to make ourselves agreeable to others through friendliness, through acquiescence to their demands, and through conformity of our conduct to their dispositions. This ground for a charming complaisance is beautiful, and the malleability of such a heart is kindly. Yet it is so far from being a virtue that unless higher principles set bounds for it and weaken it, all sorts of vices may spring from it....for he does not act in accordance of the rules of good conduct in general, but rather in accordance with an inclination that is beautiful in itself but which in so far as it is without self-control and without principles becomes ridiculous.

Thus true virtue can only be grafted upon principles, and it will become more sublime and noble the more general they are....I believe I can bring all this together if I say that it is the feeling of the beauty and the dignity of human nature. The first is a ground of universal affection, the second of universal respect, and if this feeling had the greatest perfection in any human heart then this human being would certainly love and value himself, but only in so far as he is one among all to whom his widespread and noble feeling extends itself. Only when one subordinates one's own particular inclination to such an enlarged one can our kindly drives be proportionately applied and bring about the noble attitude that is the beauty of virtue."

Kant, *Observations on the Feeling of the Beautiful and the Sublime*,
1764 (Trans. by John Richardson)

"The relations between individuals in the several situations to which the substance is particularised for their *ethical duties*. The ethical personality, i.e., the subjectivity which is permeated by the substantial life, is *virtue*. In relation to the bare facts of external being, to *destiny*, virtue does not treat them as a mere negation, and is thus a quiet repose in itself: in relation to substantial objectivity, to the total of ethical actuality, it exists as confidence, as deliberate work for the community, and the capacity of sacrificing self thereto; while in relation to the incidental relations of social circumstance, it is in the first instance justice, and then benevolence. In the latter sphere, and in its attitude to its own visible being and corporeity, the individuality expresses its special character, temperament, etc. as personal *virtues*."

Hegel, *The Phenomenology of Spirit*, 1807 (Trans. by William Wallace)

"But there is this basis of powerful natural sentiment; and this it is which, when once the general happiness is recognized as the ethical standard, will constitute the strength of the utilitarian morality. This firm foundation is that of the social feelings of mankind; the desire to be in unity with our fellow creatures, which is already a powerful principle in human nature, and happily one of those which tend to become stronger, even without express inculcation, from the influences of advancing civilization. The social state is at once so natural, so necessary, and so habitual to man, that, except in some unusual circumstances or by an effort of voluntary abstraction, he never conceives himself otherwise than as a member of a body; and this association is riveted more and more, as mankind are further removed from the state of savage independence. Any condition, therefore, which is essential to a state of society, becomes more and more an inseparable part of every person's conception of the state of things which he is born into, and which is the destiny of a human being. Now, society between human beings, except in the relation of master and slave, is manifestly impossible on any other footing than that the interests of all are to be consulted. Society between equals can only exist on the understanding that the interests of all are to be regarded equally. And since in all states of civilization, every person, except an absolute monarch, has equals, every one is obliged to live on these terms with somebody; and in every age some advance is made towards a state in which it will be impossible to live permanently on other terms with anybody. In this way people grow up unable to conceive as possible to them a state of total disregard of other people's interests. They are under a necessity of conceiving themselves as at least abstaining from all the grosser injuries, and (if only for their own protection.) living in a state of constant protest against them. They are also familiar with the fact of co-operating with others, and proposing to themselves a collective, not an individual, interest, as the aim (at least for the time being) of their actions. So long as they are co-operating, their ends are identified with those of others; there is at least a temporary feeling that the interests of others are their own interests. Not only does all strengthening of social ties, and all healthy growth of society, give to each individual a stronger personal interest in practically consulting the welfare of others; it also leads him to identify his feelings more and more with their good, or at least with an ever greater degree of practical consideration for it. He comes, as though instinctively, to be conscious of himself as a being who *of course* pays regard to others. The good of others becomes to him a thing naturally and necessarily to be attended to, like any of the physical conditions of our existence. Now, whatever amount of this feeling a person has, he is urged by the strongest motives both of interest and of sympathy to demonstrate it, and to the utmost of his power encourage it in others; and even if he has none of it himself, he is as greatly interested as any one else that others should have it. Consequently, the smallest germs of the feeling are laid hold of and nourished by the contagion of sympathy and the influences of education; and a complete web of corroborative association is woven round it, by the powerful agency of the external sanctions. This mode of conceiving ourselves and human life, as civilization goes on, is felt to be more and more natural. Every step in political improvement renders it more so, by removing the sources of opposition of interest, and levelling those inequalities of legal privilege between individuals or classes, owing to which there are large portions of mankind whose happiness it is still practicable to disregard. In an improving state of the human mind, the influences are constantly on the increase, which tend to generate in each individual a feeling of unity with all the rest; which feeling, if perfect, would make him never think of, or desire, any beneficial condition for himself, in the benefits of which they are not included."

John Stuart Mill, *Utilitarianism,* **1863**

"Since everything which is demanded is by that fact a good, must not the guiding principle for ethical philosophy (since all demands conjointly cannot be satisfied in this poor world) be simply to satisfy at all times *as many demands as we can?* That act must be the best act, accordingly, which makes for the *best whole*, in the sense of awakening the least sum of dissatisfactions. In the casuistic scale, therefore, those ideals must be written highest which *prevail at the least cost,* or by whose realization the least possible number of other ideals are destroyed. Since victory and defeat there must be, the victory to the philosophically prayed for is that of the more inclusive side - of the side which even in the hour of triumph will to some degree do justice to the ideals in which the vanquished party's interests lay. The course of history is nothing but the story of men's struggles from generation to generation to find the more and more inclusive order."

William James, *The Moral Philosopher and the Moral Life,* **1891**

"In intellectual disciplines and in the enjoyment of art and nature we discover value in our ability to forget self, to be realistic, to perceive justly. We use our imagination not to escape the world but to join it, and this exhilarates us because of the distance between our ordinary dulled consciousness and an apprehension of the real. The value concepts are here patently tied on to the world, they are stretched as it were between the truth-seeking mind and the world, they are not moving about on their own as adjuncts of the personal will. The authority of the morals is the authority of truth, that is of reality. We can see the length, the extension, of these concepts at patient attention transforms accuracy without interval into just discernment. Here too we can see it as natural to the particular kind of creatures that we are that love should be inseparable from justice, and clear vision from respect for the real.

"That virtue operates in exactly the same kind of way in the central area of morality is less easy to perceive. Human beings are far more complicated and enigmatic and ambiguous than languages or mathematical concepts, and selfishness operates in a much more devious and frenzied manner in our relations with them. Ignorance, muddle, fear, wishful thinking, lack of tests often make us feel that moral choice is something arbitrary, a matter for personal will rather than for attentive study. Our attachments tend to be selfish and strong, and the transformation of our loves from selfishness to unselfishness is sometimes hard even to conceive of. Yet is the situation really so different? Should a retarded child be kept at home or sent to an institution? Should an elderly relation who is a trouble-maker be cared for or asked to go away? Should an unhappy marriage be continued for the sake of the children? Should I leave my family in order to do political work? Should I neglect them in order to practice my art? The love which brings the right answer is an exercise of justice and realism and really *looking*. The difficulty is to keep the attention fixed upon the real situation and to prevent it from returning surreptitiously to the self with consolations of self-pity, resentment, fantasy and despair...."

Iris Murdoch, *The Sovereignty of Good Over Other Concepts***, Leslie Stephen Lecture, 1967**

"The oppressor is solidary with the oppressed only when he stops regarding the oppressed as an abstract category and sees them as persons who have been unjustly dealt with, deprived of their voice, cheated in the sale of their labor - when he stops making pious, sentimental and individualistic gestures and risks an act of love. True solidarity is found only in the plenitude of this act of love, in its existentiality, in its praxis. To affirm that men and women are person and as persons should be free, and yet to do nothing tangible to make this affirmation a reality, is a farce."

Paulo Freire, *Pedagogy of the Oppressed***, Continuum International Publishing Group, 1970 (Trans. by Myra Bergman Ramos)**

"This religious orientation does not basically change the definition of universal principles of human justice found at moral Stage 6, but it integrates these principles with a perspective on life's ultimate meaning. One part of the notion of a 'Stage 7' comes from Erikson's discussion of an ultimate stage in the life cycle in which integrity is found and despair ultimately confronted. Even awareness of universal principles of justice, typically attained young adulthood, does not remove the possibility of despair; indeed, it may enhance the sense of difficulty of finding justice in the world. As we would phrase the problem, after attaining a clear awareness of universal ethical principles valid against the usual skeptical doubts there still remains the loudest skeptical doubt of all: "Why be moral? Why be just, in a universe that is largely unjust?" At this level, the answer to the question "Why be moral?" entails the question "Why live?" and the parallel question, "How face death?" Thus, ultimate moral maturity requires a mature solution to the question of the meaning of life. This, in turn, we argue, is hardly a moral question *per se*; it is an ontological or religious one. Not only is the question not a moral one, but it is also not a question resolvable on purely logical or rational grounds. Nevertheless, we use a metaphorical notion of a 'Stage 7' to suggest some meaningful solutions to this question that are compatible with rational universal ethics. The characteristics of all these solutions is that they involve contemplative experience of a nondualistic variety. The logic of such experience is sometimes expressed in theistic terms of union with God, but it need not be. Its essence is the sense of being a part of the whole of life and the adoption of a cosmic, as opposed to a universal, humanistic Stage 6 perspective.

....In the state of mind we have metaphorically termed Stage 7 we identify ourselves with the cosmic or infinite perspective itself; we value life from its standpoint. At such a time, what is ordinarily background becomes foreground and the self is no longer figure to ground. We sense the unity of the whole and ourselves as part of that unity. This experience of unity, often mistakenly treated as a mere rush of mystic feelings, is at 'Stage 7' associated with a structure of ontological and moral conviction."

Lawrence Kohlberg, *Essays on Moral Development, Vol 1,* **Harper & Row, 1981**

"When asked 'What does responsibility mean to you?' a high school student replied: 'Responsibility means making a commitment and then sticking to it.' This response confirms the common understanding of responsibility as personal commitment and contractual obligation. A different conception of the self and of morality appears, however, in another student's reply: 'Responsibility is when you are aware of others and you are aware of their feelings.... Responsibility is taking charge of yourself by looking at others around you and seeing what they need and seeing what you need...and then taking the initiative.' In this construction, responsibility means acting responsively in relationships, and the self - as a moral agent - takes the initiative to gain awareness and respond to the perception of need.....

These two conceptions of responsibility, illustrated here by the definitions of two young women, were heard initially as a dissonance between women's voices and psychological theories (Gilligan, 1982). Exploring this dissonance, I defined new categories of moral judgment and self-description to capture the experience of connection or interdependence, which overrides the traditional contrast between egoism and altruism. This enlarged conceptual framework provides a new way of listening to differences not only between but also within the thinking of women and men. In a series of studies designed to investigate the relationships between conceptions of self and morality and to test their association with gender and age, two moral voices could reliably be distinguished in the way people framed and resolved moral problems and in their evaluations of choices they made. One voice speaks of connection, not hurting, care and response; and one speaks of equality, reciprocity, justice, and rights. Although both voices regularly appeared in conjunction, a tension between them was suggested by the confusion that marked their intersection and also by the tendency for one voice to predominate...."

Carol Gilligan, *Mapping the Moral Domain*, **President and Fellows of Harvard College, 1988**

Across the ages, the same pattern repeats itself: thoughts and actions that facilitate harmony, kindness and togetherness, that perpetuate mutually caring relationship above and beyond obligation or self-interest, are described with the highest moral regard. And yet these insights are trapped within a self-referential loop; such characteristics are only moral because, well, we deem them to be moral. From a second order, meta-ethics perspective, we would have to agree with J.L. Mackie that there may indeed be *agreed-upon* moral values, but not really objective or absolute ones. And here we encounter our first major hurdle, for the moment we begin to define moral development in any way, we project a presupposed values hierarchy onto that model. There is no escaping this. In and of themselves, morals express a standard of intention and action that may be "noble" in an abstract sense (and, at least for Aristotle, approved of by the gods), *but why is it noble?* The agreement of such diverse thinkers over the ages is significant in generating a standard of reference for moral thought and conduct, but what justifies conformance to that standard?

Well, it turns out that nearly all of these thinkers agree, either explicitly or implicitly, on a common root: one's capacity for love. This love is not an unfocused or shallow warmth, nor is it a reflexive duty, but rather a deeply felt commitment to the happiness and well-being of others. In this lineage, that orientation is frequently referred to as *agape* - what Kohlberg aptly describes as "responsible love." In a utilitarian sense, *agape* contributes to social cohesion; it helps bind society into functional structures, facilitating collective agreement on standards of behavior, which in turn establish a baseline of mutual trust and benefit. But within *agape's* utility are impulses that transcend self-interest. As Sidgwick writes in *The Methods of Ethics*:

> "On the one hand it is of course true, that when those whom we love are pleased or pained, we ourselves feel sympathetic pleasure and pain: and further, that the flow of love or kindly feeling is itself highly pleasurable. So that it is at least plausible to interpret the benevolent impulse as aiming ultimately at the attainment of one or both of these two kinds of pleasures, or at the averting of sympathetic pain. But we may observe, first, that the impulse to beneficent action produced in us by sympathy is often so much out

of proportion to any actual consciousness of sympathetic pleasure and pain in ourselves, that it would be paradoxical to regard this latter as its object. Often indeed we cannot but feel that a tale of actual suffering arouses in us an excitement on the whole more pleasurable than painful, like the excitement of witnessing a tragedy; and yet at the same time stirs in us an impulse to relieve it, even when the process of relieving is painful and laborious and involves various sacrifices of our own pleasures. Again, we may often free ourselves from sympathetic pain most easily by merely turning our thoughts from the external suffering that causes it: and we sometimes feel an egoistic impulse to do this, which we can then distinguish clearly from the properly sympathetic impulse prompting us to relieve the original suffering.   And finally, the much-commended pleasures of benevolence seem to require, in order to be felt in any considerable degree, the pre-existence of a desire to do good to others for their sakes and not for our own. As Hutcheson explains, we may cultivate benevolent affection for the sake of the pleasures attending it (just as the gourmand cultivates appetite), but we cannot produce it at will, however strong may be our desire of these pleasures: and when it exists, even though it may owe its origin to a purely egoistic impulse, it is still essentially a desire to do good to others for their sake and not for our own."

Again, however, although formulations of a love-centered morality unify this lineage of Western thought, we must still recognize them to be a product of imagination. Even the assumption that a humanizing, liberating or socially binding function is a desirable utility is, well, a consequence of our moral creativity. If we accept the belief that a cohesive and compassionate society, a just and moral society, is desirable and worthwhile, we tend to assign moral weight to this belief. So it follows that the degree to which we are willing to invest in society - from the perspective of embracing collective responsibilities - may depend on our relationship with that basic assumption, the quality of our imagination, our capacity for love, and whatever innate proclivities we possess to make such an investment. In essence, it will depend not only on the quality and quantity of affection for our fellow human beings, but also on our creative capacities for expression. This is as much an inclination as a choice, and yet we cannot take it for granted; all of this suggests we should approach our moral compass as consciously as possible, and decide for ourselves whether this particular lineage resonates with our own ideals.

Are there other lineages to consider? There are probably hundreds, some of which take an entirely different direction regarding moral function, promoting alternate values hierarchies and different meta-ethical assumptions. As one example, when we remove the ground of loving kindness, we suddenly find ourselves in new territory, and indeed an entirely different heritage of Western thought. We encounter frames like nihilism, egoistic hedonism, Epicureanism and Randian objectivism, where the primary aims of individuals and society are the facilitation of pleasure, unfettered free will, or narrowly defined self-interest. These may become equated with "virtue" to the neglect of many of the other moral concepts enumerated in the love-based lineage; in fact, anything hinting at egalitarianism, benevolence or altruism is sometimes forcefully rejected. As examples, Hobbes and Nietzsche might regard such constructs as contrived by society to corral a naturally brutal or amoral human animal - such aspirations would be imposed or persuaded conventions rather than innate impulses or self-evident virtues.

Unfortunately for Nietzsche and Hobbes, neuroscience has begun to show us that many prosocial ethical responses are hardwired into our neurobiology, and that what we believe to be rational considerations, objective self-interest or even conditioned social mores may have far less relevance in our choices than those neurological structures (see the research of Grit Hein, Scott Huettel, Ralph Adolphs or Antonio Damasio for examples). The evolutionary biologist Marc Hauser goes on to assert that our neurobiology is actually genetically predisposed to acquire a universal moral grammar. Moreover, empathic complexity, sociality, and other precursors to moral constructs are readily observable in many primates and other species, as the work of Frans de Waal and Barbara King have extensively explored. And if we entertain Edward O. Wilson's hypothesis - or even Leslie Stephen's ideas in *The Science of Ethics* a century earlier - this social cohesion has provided a critical evolutionary advantage throughout the emergence of homo sapiens; an advantage that, it could be argued, would be existentially risky for us to abandon.

Still, is social cohesion a worthwhile objective? It does facilitate the peaceful coordination of society, and the basic survival of our species, but it also inspires loving kindness between human beings and refines the skillfulness of that loving kindness. This, in turn, leads to a much richer, creative and multidimensional flourishing for all, a thriving that seems essential for intellectual, emotional, cultural and spiritual complexity and advancement; that is, for multidimensional evolution and the enlargement of consciousness. This evolutionary complex can then provide our meta-ethical justification for a consistent values hierarchy; we are still trapped in a self-referential loop, but one that marries pragmatism, love and art.

Thus I find many alternate-lineage philosophies - those that do not recognize this evolutionary complexity - self-limiting, fractured and unimaginative, excluding far too many critical dimensions in pursuit of a few confining principles (the idea that there are no moral principles being just one such confining principle). They also reflect a paucity of love. So where, for example, Carol Gilligan divided morality into caring-based and justice-based relations, these other perspectives might discard both in favor of either self-indulgent egoism or fearful legalism, viewing harmonious human relations as a means to an end, rather than an end in itself. Such philosophies are, in essence, less socially developed, perhaps demonstrating a reduced emotional intelligence; where love is absent, there is far less creativity. From a neurobiological perspective, perhaps these philosophies are the result of structural deficiencies in the brain. In this light there is a nature/nurture question with respect to individual moral choices; it seems likely that our neurobiological proclivities would cause us to seek out reinforcing actions and ideologies. In any case, when I read folks like John Locke, Ayn Rand, Murray Rothbard or Milton Friedman I find this monodimensionality reflected in their views.

Some thinkers have also attempted to similarly constrain or eliminate moral considerations in defining "rational" social interactions - such as John Rawls in *A Theory of Justice* - and have consequently arrived at principles that facilitate self-interest or social cohesion, while not completely rejecting a broader vocabulary of moral thought and action. My readings of G.E. Moore or Elizabeth Anscombe seem to drift along this particular thought stream as well. As already mentioned, there are probably hundreds more lineages to examine, but I sense they fall into two camps: those that advocate a broad moral function and creativity, grounded in a felt experience of affectionate compassion with outcomes akin to Aristotle's virtue ethics, and those that confine moral function to more simplistic impulses, grounded mainly in egoism, fear or hyperrationality (by which I mean overemphasizing what is rational to the exclusion of other input streams). This is equally true among postmodern, relativistic "little narratives" where morality is negotiated within each community or culture; there need not be an all-inclusive narrative of principled morality to achieve an Aristotelian breadth of virtues, only an underlying current of skillfully compassionate affection, which will lead to very similar, if not identical, results. Likewise, if love is absent, those little narratives are likely to correspond with an alternate lineage of hyperrationality, egoism or fear.

As examples of a broader consistency, we should also consider non-Western lineages. So far I have focused on Western philosophies because the dominant political economy currently enveloping the globe happens to be rooted in Western memeplexes, and I find it particularly fascinating that expressions of market-centric capitalism are so often at odds with what, until very recently, has been the West's predominant moral lineage. As will become clear in later chapters, it's almost as if cognitive dissonance was deliberately engineered into our political economy. When we look further afield, among the great Eastern wisdom traditions, we find many of the same sentiments as those championed by the Aristotelian camp. For example, in Buddhism, the "perfections" (*pāramitā*) adherents aim for include generosity, morally disciplined conduct, diligence, patience and tolerance, transcendent wisdom, truthfulness, skillfulness and serenity. The sublime attitudes or "four immeasurables" (*brahmavihāras*) of Buddhism include loving kindness toward all (*maitri*), mercy and compassion for those who suffer (*karunā*), empathetic joy for others without envy (*mudita*), and equanimity in any circumstance (*upekṣā*). In Hinduism, what it means to "act in accordance with *dharma*" varies from person to person, from caste to caste, and according one's stage of life (*ashrama*), but always entails loving kindness towards all living beings (*ahimsa:* "the avoidance of violence"), and generating positive *karma* by practicing, well, *dharma*. Although its variations of meaning are nearly as diverse as its practitioners, *dharma* essentially means "ethical conduct" with respect to others, society and one's own salvation (*moksha*). In reading through Jewish, Sufi and Taoist texts, as well as the literature of many other spiritual traditions from around the globe, we find subtle variations on the same central theme of how to be skillfully compassionate in humble and selfless ways.

So although we cannot assert a universal definition of moral creativity for all of humanity, there is certainly a strong resonance between many - if not most - of the diverse cultural perspectives offered around the world and throughout the ages. There is a common thread of themes, intentions, actions and outcomes that transcends and unifies their intertextuality. Of course, this resonance could simply mean that the impulse to elaborate on human virtue issues from similar personality types wherever they happen to reside, in the same way that there are likely folks who enjoy hitting people with clubs for fun in virtually every culture, but who don't happen to record their moral vision for posterity in the same fashion. Perhaps the act of writing itself evokes a specific family of sentiments by activating certain parts of the brain, and thereby distorts unrecorded actualities. Like the self-referential loop of projected values, there really isn't any objective way to establish an absolute truth here; we can only observe, experience, experiment, ruminate and meditate, then compare our insights to achieve an intersubjective median that balances all accounts.

For me personally, moral creativity grounded in love is a powerful, productive force. It doesn't matter that my own values hierarchies may only be the product of my imagination, because virtuous thoughts and actions are so clearly self-justifying. Observing with delight how character traits like being just, generous, courageous, moderate, self-sacrificing or self-disciplined invigorate and sustain all kinds of loving relationship firmly implants the desire to perfect those traits in myself. It is their dynamic utility across multiple dimensions of being that fascinates me, compelling me to expand my moral ideals and vocabulary rather than reducing or limiting them in any way. I also believe there is also a mystical (supramental, transcendent, unmanifest) element to moral intentionality that affirms moral creativity when we engage it within spiritual perception-cognition. We need only practice various meditative techniques to affirm a permeating compassion that blossoms through mystical insight (see my *Essential*

Mysticism for further discussion of this). However, love doesn't require validation beyond itself, because its benefits are self-evident. As Politinus wrote in the *First Ennead*: "If a fire is to warm something else, must there be a fire to warm that fire?"

So I yearn to enhance the breadth, texture and color of my moral imagination because I perceive how people flourish when operating within that thought field - even though I don't fully comprehend what the mechanisms of that flourishing are. Perhaps, in part, it is the quality of mind, heart and spirit that result from living in integrity with such ideals. Perhaps it is witnessing the resulting joy and happiness in others. Perhaps it is the engineering of a deeper, more enduring interpersonal trust than might otherwise be available. Perhaps it is the astounding unity of multiplicities, the harmony of mind, heart, body and spirit, that spontaneously arises when loving virtues are exercised. Perhaps it is the intuition that something greater than the sum of its parts is being synthesized, or that something transcendent or previously unmanifest is being reified. Whatever it may be, the generation and application of an all-inclusive moral creativity has had me in its thrall since I graduated from an anxiety-ridden, existentialist adolescence.

Moral creativity could also be described as "broad-spectrum moral synthesis," a product of multiple intelligences within - emotional, social, spiritual, somatic, analytic - working in unison. A moral choice can be viewed as the synthesis of all of these input streams, and the breadth of our moral vocabulary as dependent on how readily we can access and integrate these dimensions of perception-cognition. For those with a limited moral vocabulary, a rigid, black-and-white, rules-oriented assessment is a safe and reliable haven for moral judgments. But the more developed our moral creativity - and the more it is infused with skillfully compassionate affection - the more we will extrapolate subtle, nuanced, multidimensional criteria that are context-sensitive, variable and graduated. Beyond shades of gray, moral insight becomes a function of rich and vibrant colors across the full spectrum of human perspectives, experiences, motivations and responses. How often do we find ourselves mistaken in our judgments regarding someone's actions, only because we did not have all the relevant facts from their perspective? This is one of many routine proofs that a morality grounded in limited information is an underdeveloped morality, and why integrating as many dimensions of understanding as possible is crucial to making wise decisions.

So then, when operating from the vantage point of moral creativity, what are the goals of economic, cultural and political systems and institutions? This is where things get interesting, because the aims of society become as rich and multifaceted as human imagination itself. Within Integral Lifework, those aims are informed by twelve nourishment centers, sixteen fulfillment impulses, and four primary drives. These in turn are guided by a particular frame of moral development and its strata of progression. And all of this is energized and focused by an overarching intentionality - a meta-morality or ethical superstructure - that projects a specific, driving principle underlying all moral creativity into future-oriented processes. We will be expanding on all of this shortly, but first let's return to our conception of property, then see if we can begin to resolve the tension between individual freedom and collective responsibility in a satisfying way.

Property Position in Different Political Economies

In order to break this down into digestible pieces, let's begin with just one axis of our *property matrix*: the *ownership* categorizations of *potential* property, *private* property, *communal* property, *public domain* property, *common* property, *sacred* property and *wild things*. Here is a brief overview of some approaches to the *ownership* variable in contemporary political economies:

- Marxism, in most of its state-centric (Marxist-Leninist) manifestations, has concentrated property *ownership* in the *public domain*, aggressively reassigning *private*, *sacred* and other forms of property to that category and opposing many forms of exclusive *ownership* as a component of economic productivity. Marx and Engels initially advocated proletariat empowerment and classless society via pluralistic democracy, and more specifically via direct democracy ("universal suffrage") as exemplified in the Paris Commune. But Lenin expanded the "dictatorship of the proletariat" into a much more limited single-party state that annihilated divergent perspectives through violent oppression. In the case of the U.S.S.R., this state-centric model did not survive the inefficiencies of corruption, unpopular domestic policies, and a deliberate confrontation with U.S.-style capitalism that led to costly proxy wars. Some remaining non-pluralistic, state-centric Marxist-Leninist examples are China, Cuba, Laos, and Vietnam. China's recent experiments with free enterprise zones have led to a hybridization of *public domain* and *private* property, but retained an emphasis on centralized state controls backed by single-party authoritarianism. So far, China's hybrid model and enthusiastic participation in the global marketplace has been more successful than the former Soviet Union's oppositional approach, though increasing state-sanctioned environmental degradation, corruption and classism threaten to undermine China's economic success.

- The U.S.-style, market-centric mixed economy, one of the most influential and expansive political economies to date, elevates *private* property as the primary driver of commerce. As a result, a constant pressure to privatize most other categories of property becomes an overwhelming force in capitalism. However, the U.S. also recognizes the importance of *public domain* property, such as transportation and communication systems, to facilitate the trading of *private* property and for other pubic benefit. In addition, a variant of *sacred* property can still be found in monuments, parks and artifacts protected for natural, cultural and historic preservation purposes. The concept of *communal* property also exists in various forms as worker-owned or member-owned cooperatives. Contrastingly, *communal* property has also been defined through publicly traded companies, where shareholders with the most shares can directly influence, and benefit from, the economic activity of those companies.   Amid this complex mix in the U.S., the state retains significant control over all forms of property *ownership*, while still encouraging the (relatively) free exchange of *private* property. This has created both tension (such as tax rebellion and deregulation sentiments) and collusion (cronyism) between representative democratic government and free enterprise.   A lethal combination of polarized special-interest anti-pluralism, reckless government spending, lack of citizen participation, deregulation and lethargic regulatory oversight has generated enduring political and economic crises in the U.S.

A significant factor in this instability has been the ascendance of very large and wealthy corporations, legal entities increasingly imbued with a host of human rights, whose disproportionate influence has undermined democracy and the rule of law to the point where American government more resembles feudalism than representative pluralism. Corporate power has effectively enforced "elitist privatization," where a majority of *private* property (and nearly all *private* property with the highest exchange value) is controlled by the wealthiest citizens.   In some instances, such as the direct initiative process available in roughly half of U.S. states, forms of direct democracy have also been implemented. But these efforts are often distorted and manipulated by well-funded special interests, who either draft and market self-serving initiatives themselves, or aggressively oppose those that threaten their interests, countering them with a deluge of misinformation.

• There have been proposals to remold U.S.-style capitalism into a more just and compassionate system. Efforts like "conscious capitalism" and its offspring, B Corporations, are the latest incarnation of an enduring American optimism that corporate culture can be changed for the better. In a similar vein, "natural capitalism" attempts to introduce true-cost accounting for natural resources, thereby recognizing externalities usually ignored by free markets, with the hope of lessening both waste and negative impacts on those resources. And of course there are an endless series of management training and organizational development consultants who will help re-brand a company into a worker-friendly, environmentally conscious, civically constructive enterprise. None of these efforts, however, have changed the market-centric assignments of property *ownership* in the U.S. system.

• Among mixed-economies with a bit more central planning and slightly less market-centric emphasis are the pluralistic, representative, constitutional democracies of Canada and Europe. Here there are various ratios of *private, public domain,* and *communal* property arrangements, some leaning more towards centralized state control (e.g. France's presidential democracy) and some with more distributed controls (e.g. Switzerland's direct democracy). Most of these countries have parliamentary forms of government, often with a tendency toward technocratic specialization in high-level appointed positions. So far, those mixed-economy countries with robust, productive economic engines and judiciously managed state budgets have held their own within a global marketplace, even outperforming the U.S. in economic resilience (as Germany has done, for example). However, countries with weaker economic engines in combination with more pervasive corruption and lack of citizen participation have performed much more poorly (for example, Greece has a long tradition of increasing entitlements even as its tax base is eroded by widespread tax evasion).

- India is a democratic socialist system that also presents a heterogeneous mix of *private, public domain* and *communal* property. Although India is also a pluralistic representative democracy in parliamentary form, there has been a strong dynastic tradition in choosing its leaders. On the one hand, until very recently India has successfully resisted the intrusion and domination of international corporate monopolies in its markets. On the other, a combination of dynastic politics, corruption, terrorism, the caste system, the joint family structure, and constant tensions between central and local authorities, have both undermined the effectiveness of many of its state run industries, and slowed the emergence of robust capitalist enterprises. There are ongoing efforts to further liberalize the Indian economy, but whatever the resulting emphasis of a free-market/central planning mix, the underlying issues unique to India's culture present fascinating challenges to all systems of property *ownership* and trade.

- At the other extreme, in developing capitalist economies controlled by despots (autocratic, oligarchic, monarchist, etc.) the assignations of *private* and *public domain* converge to facilitate enrichment of the ruling elite; this is perhaps the most extreme case of elitist privatization.

- A number of "intentional communities" around world utilize *communal* property *ownership*, describing themselves as Ecovillages, cohousing arrangements, income-sharing communes or expense-sharing cooperatives. These intentional communities are inspired by a diverse array of ideologies, from anarchism to Christianity, and so governance runs the gamut from democratic to authoritarian. However, once again most such experiments exist within larger, market-centric or mixed environments, and most are of a fairly small scale. A directory of intentional communities can be found here: http://directory.ic.org/

- A larger scale implementation of a *communal ownership* approach can be found in various cooperative enterprises. For example, Spain's Mondragon Corporation, founded by Father José María Arizmendiarrieta, is a federation of over 250 worker-owned cooperatives, whose members number some 80,000 people. Mondragon is involved in producing everything from refrigerators to ferry boats, financial products to education, and even has its own retail chains. A helpful overview and historical data are available at http://www.mondragon-corporation.com/ENG/Who-we-are/Introduction.aspx. Globally, there are hundreds of successful worker-owned cooperatives, though none as large or diverse as Mondragon. In North America, non-profit member-owned credit unions are another thriving example of a *communal ownership* of property in a financial cooperative. Associations of such credit unions, such as Canada's Desjardins Group, offer a wide array of financial products that successfully compete with for-profit institutions. It should be noted, however, that, as with many intentional communities, these larger cooperatives are imbedded within market-centric environments. In worker cooperatives, decisions tend to be made bottom-up either by consensus, direct democracy, or representative democracy where workers elect a leader; we could conceive of these as experiments in democratic "market socialism." In member cooperatives, decisions tend to follow a more traditional top-down corporate capitalism model.

- Gift economies (sometimes referred to as "grant economies") appear to have existed throughout much of human civilization, and continue to persist in various forms as components of nearly every other approach. The almost universal characteristic of gift economies is that they treat most "gifted" property as *common* property. Gift economies tend to be the most self-organizing and least hierarchical, usually co-existing with other political economies. With advent of the Internet-dominant mediasphere, there has been an explosion of gifts in the form of creative intellectual property. In this context, there is usually a community of individuals with specialized knowledge who determine what gifts are appropriate and effective for a given application, thereby echoing technocratic decision-making to some degree. These decision-makers are often encouraged or enabled through community consensus - based on their demonstrated skills, the quality and frequency of their own contributions to the commons, and of course their willingness to participate as decision-makers. It should be noted, however, that in most cases these decision-makers are not gate-keepers for the gifting process, they are merely opinion shapers about the contributive value of each gift.

Examples of modern gift economies include the Open Source movement, Creative Commons licensing, Open Access to academic journals, and indeed much of the academic research at public institutions. The recent announcements of the Australian Research Council, the Obama Administration and others to make publicly funded research freely available to the public (within twelve months of publication) is an example of this gifting trend. Another promising development is the Global Village Construction Set (see www.opensourcecology.org), which aims to localize sustainable, self-sufficient technologies of all kinds at the individual and community level. Although reciprocation for gifts is never expected in gifting models, perpetuating the gifting process is. For example, building on previous research and releasing the results, or adding value to an existing Open Source product and sharing that freely.

Other alternatives also abound, mainly as proposed ideals, but also as experiments and potential transitions among various existing political economies. First, since recent political events in the U.S. have catapulted one flavor of this ideology to the foreground, let's take a quick look at different forms of Libertarianism:

- Market-centric Libertarianism ("Right-Libertarianism" or "Market Libertarianism") seeks to greatly attenuate or remove altogether state oversight for commercial trade, assigning as much property as possible to *private ownership* while retaining some form of democracy. Market-centric libertarians differ on the extent and role of government, some recognizing the importance of the rule of law, and others rejecting it as unnecessary or oppressive. However, market-centric Libertarian approaches have yet to be successfully employed in the real world. In the closest approximations to these models - such as the transition of former Soviet Union countries to free markets without a strong rule of law - the results have been devastating. In these and other environments where capitalism has reigned for long periods without governmental controls (as the example of Somalia was for many years), what little wealth is generated is inevitably concentrated in a select and usually criminally brutal few. Meanwhile, nearly everyone else in those societies suffers increasing deprivation, poverty, abuse and exploitation. Despite the lack of empirical support, market-centric Libertarianism has gained popularity in U.S. public discourse, and currently maintains a strong association with the "Libertarian Party" political brand (see www.lp.org for confirmation of this trend).

- Libertarian Socialism ("Left-Libertarianism") generally opposes *private* property *ownership*, and considers a majority of property to be in either the *public domain* or *common* property categories. I say either/or because it follows that if privatization is not possible in a given system, then there is no need to exclude property from privatization by controlling it as a *public domain* resource that is protected by the state; thus there would be a tendency to ultimately treat all property as *common*. Libertarian socialism in fact opposes governmental authority, and resists the perpetuation of civic institutions that wield power over citizens. Therefore, many forms of anarchism, communalism and autonomism fit neatly within this ideology. In most Libertarian socialist proposals, all collective decisions would be achieved via decentralized/distributed forms of a more direct democracy. Noam Chomsky (one of my favorite thinkers) is a vocal proponent of this approach.

As one specific example, Participism is a form of Libertarian socialism proposed by Michael Albert and Robin Hahnel. In its participatory economics (Parecon), participism assigns as much property as possible to *common*. The Participist political structure (Parpolity) consists of nested councils, beginning with small local groups that operate on consensus, with the underlying principle that anyone affected by a given decision be allowed input into such a decision. Although Participism in particular has gained some traction in public discourse over the last decade, it is important to appreciate that Libertarian socialism is a parent to hundreds of distinct ideologies.

As of yet, Libertarian socialism has not been implemented on a large scale. However, Elinor Ostrom and others have documented small scale examples around the globe that evolved spontaneously (see Elinor Ostrom's research on "common pool resource management" for more). Because of their scale, however, these examples tend to treat property *communally* in relation to the larger systems within which they are embedded.

Over the past fifty years there has also been an increasing trend to promote low-impact, renewable, ecologically sustainable approaches in human interactions with the Earth. Strategies address everything from industry, agriculture and architecture to city planning, as well as various systems of production and resource management. A consistent theme throughout most of these proposals is an increased valuation and prioritization of all natural species and systems in various ways, reversing centuries of Nature's subordination to human wants, whims and destructive activity. Some examples of this philosophical orientation are Deep Ecology, Biocentrism and Ecosophy. Closely related philosophies, such as Ecofeminism and Ecotheology, also touch on the need to revise social structures and relationships that have distorted human interactions with Nature, and human interactions with other humans, in similar ways.

In practice, attempts to shape the direction of political economy with eco-centric tools come in many forms. There are efforts such as the Earth Economics think tank, which consults with businesses, policy makers, governments and NGOs to generate ecologically sustainable solutions for economies of all scales. There are initiatives such as Ecovillages springing up around the globe that embody eco-centric models on scales from small communities (Findhorn, Fryers Forest) to envisioned cities (Auroville). There is also the proposal of Ecological Keynesianism that relies on state-centric realignment of political economies to a more eco-centric model. And there are movements, such as Permaculture and Transition Towns, that seek to percolate eco-centric practices up through existing political economies via local grass roots activism. Because the fundamental values are so similar, cross pollination among all of these approaches is common.

In a majority of eco-centric visions, the *private, public domain* and *communal* property categories tend to conform to the political economy in which a particular flavor of eco-centrism arises. There may be an emphasis on changing attitudes and consumption habits on a personal level, such as advocating local food or goods sourcing, using alternative energy, supporting small enterprise rather than big corporations, etc. Or the focus may be eco-friendly planning and resource utilization on an organizational, business practice, community or municipal development level. Beyond this, there is state-enforced abandonment of ecologically destructive energy, technology and industry in favor of Green solutions, which is increasingly explored in places like Germany. But all such strategies still leave most of the status quo property categorizations pretty much in place. The only substantive exceptions seem to be Ecovillages that intentionally alter their internal economy to a more self-sufficient *communal* and *public domain* property orientation - for example, Eco-Communalism. As is the case with other intentional communities, of course, these experiments are usually still embedded within market-centric systems.

However, what eco-centric strategies do differently than most other approaches is encourage us to change our relationship with *potential* property, *common* property, and *wild things* in particular. For example, eco-centrism challenges the assumption of capitalism that *potential* property should become *private* property, and even that certain *wild things* should ever be considered *potential* property at all. Instead, it elevates some *wild things* to the *sacred* category and exempts them from trade (for example, Permaculture's "Zone 5"). Also, because of the focus on self-sufficiency and sustainability, there is a deliberate effort to shift certain kinds of *private* and *public domain* property outside of routine commerce. Produce harvested a long distance from the community, for example, or services offered by companies who aren't ecologically responsible, or even benevolent government assistance, may all be resisted as part of a commitment to *communal* resources that align with eco-centric values. What is perhaps most striking in eco-centric proposals is that when *common* or *public domain* property is defined "for the benefit of all," that "all" includes the natural realm itself; in other words, human activity tends to be managed specifically with some benefit to Nature in mind.

Contrastingly, in market-centric mixed economies, capitalism has a very different impact on *common* property, *potential* property and *wild things*. In these systems, dependency on perpetual growth insists as much property as possible be defined as *private* to enable trade that benefits stakeholders (investors, owners, etc.). The constant, sometimes desperate privatizing impulse constantly seeks inroads into other categories of property. In the U.S., this has precipitated the decline of *public domain* property in particular. For example, the FCC reassigning public broadcast frequencies to private wireless companies; the private exploitation of mineral, oil and timber resources on public lands; the substantial profits pharmaceutical companies routinely generate from publicly funded drug research, and so on. But this same pressure also seeks to appropriate any newly discovered *potential* property as private property as well; this is such an aggressive tendency that whole new worlds of property are routinely invented to satisfy the need. Along these lines, anything that may have once been considered *common* property and beyond reach - even ice caps and ocean, airspace and atmosphere - is increasingly redefined as *private* property to facilitate commerce. Even what could be considered the "social commons" is being appropriated as well. And of course *wild things*, in the form of various naturally occurring species of plant and animal (or their natural byproducts), are also subject to privatization. In a market-centric system, property exists mainly for those with capital - that is, those who can benefit directly from trade - and the natural realm only enters this calculation as an "unlimited" resource, rather than a stakeholder. Keeping this trend in mind, it seems clear that, in proposals like market-centric Libertarianism, a constant pressure to privatize that is unconstrained by the rule of law would eventually subjugate or destroy everything it touches.

In democratic mixed-economies with more central planning, the aggressive hunger to privatize *potential* and *common* property is less pernicious. However, both *potential* property and *common* property may be designated *public domain* in order to insulate them from capitalist appropriation. Otherwise, there appears to be less motivation to seek out new *potential* property for assignment, or to selectively grant or restrict the benefits of *common* property. In state-centric Marxist-Leninist systems, the imperative to concentrate control of property often results in assigning *potential* and *common* property to state oversight as *public domain* property. In many ways, this totalitarian reflex has had the same desperate qualities as privatization in capitalist systems; while disconnected from "market-driven" objectives, it still smacks of an elitist consolidation of power and wealth. Likewise in despotic regimes utilizing capitalism, this same control impulse may aggressively appropriate *common* and *potential* property for the benefit of the ruling class as a furtherance of elitist privatization.

In gift economies, not only is there no *private* property, but the natural course of a gift economy will convert what would otherwise be *potential* property of any utility into *common* property. *Common* property naturally resists consignment to other categories since it already embodies a "for the benefit of all" condition. Among most Libertarian socialist proposals, since the aim is generally to resist privatization, it follows that *potential* property, *common* property and *wild things* would tend to retain their native state. Most worker cooperatives (or other *communal* property enterprises) simply follow the law of the land where they reside.

Although it is not exhaustive, this account does offer a general overview of influential trends in political economic thought and practice. Once again, it should be noted that most of these approaches are either embedded in, or are in competition with, the more prevalent market-centric economies. Really this is a second major hurdle, because stepping outside of capitalistic enculturation is extremely difficult. Our understanding of exchange systems, societal organization, the role of civic institutions, the positive and negative capabilities of trade, and even our individual and cultural identities are intimately enveloped in market-centric, commercialist, corporationist assumptions. Some of the most influential cultural events of the past hundred years have been mainly a reaction to market-centric capitalism, or a result of competition between capitalism and other visions of political economy. Even the recent Occupy and TEA Party movements in the U.S. have pivoted around the central questions of modern economics; the main talking points of the 2012 U.S. Presidential election were similarly rooted in the relationships between government, free enterprise, corporate power and individual freedom. So any attempts to formulate "outsider" alternatives to the status quo are understandably daunting efforts, and may in fact be impossible without vacating capitalist assumptions entirely. In many ways, validation of "post-scarcity" alternatives will probably have to occur after capitalism's reign has come to its natural end.

However, despite this second speed bump, I still think escaping a market-centric, commercialist and corporationist system is worth a try. And so we must propose some practical transitions.

So far, we have only discussed the *ownership* axis of the *property matrix*. What about the other two? I have already suggested that more and more property is being created within the higher OSI *abstraction* layers, perhaps more than any time in human history. And I suspect that this trend will accelerate, probably exponentially. This has two independent but equally significant impacts. The first is that our institutions have really struggled, and will continue to struggle in extraordinary ways, with ownership and control of highly abstract property. As utilization and correlating valuation of property in the uppermost OSI layers becomes increasingly *common*, the inefficiencies and failures of these institutions in relating to this property will only become amplified. There is perhaps no better example of this than the fascination with social media today, with frenzied attempts to shoehorn that phenomenon into existing models of profit generation. The misunderstanding of these new "markets" of higher-layer property is also probably what led to the dot-com bubble of the late 1990s, and we will likely see similar fiascos repeated. That is, unless we change our relationship with property, advancing that relationship into a more sophisticated moral orientation.

The second impact of the higher OSI *abstraction* layer property renaissance is that those with advanced facility in higher layers do not always understand the dependencies on lower layer property - or appreciate how differently those lower layers tend to function. As I have read through various proposals of alternate political economies, imminent revolutions, and emphatic warnings from those who live and breathe mainly in these higher OSI layers, what becomes evident is that few of their proposals can be soundly applied to the *physical, data link* and *network layers* of the *abstraction* model. It's almost as if they assume the foundations upon which advanced civilization is built will just take care of themselves, when in reality the wonderfully diverse, widely distributed and relatively autonomous contributions to modern culture operating in the *session layer* would collapse into nothing without the more homogenous, hierarchical, centralized structures that support them. The Internet and greater mediasphere are potent examples of this, but education, scientific research, and in fact most major industries are similarly reliant on roads, transportation systems, power grids and communication infrastructure. It is impossible to escape this interdependency, especially as more and more subtle specialization occurs, which is why we see a very similar arrangement of OSI layers in most political economies. Yes, there are wonderful experiments at the *session layer* that focus more on the upwards dependencies (i.e a descent, as it were, of the *application layer* into the session layer), but they do not yet operate independently of their downward dependencies. We may not live by bread alone, but we still need bread.

Where we have more variation is in how the *holistic value* of property manifests in different political economies. Remember that this includes the aggregate use value of property (i.e. its esteem, desirability and dependence), in combination with its contribution to "effective, balanced nourishment." Although we have yet to fully define what effective, balanced nourishment precisely is, we can nevertheless identify some of the more potent patterns in various systems and institutions - using fuzzy assumptions that quickly become clarified.

- In Marxist-Leninist approaches with single-party, authoritative state-centrism, awareness of *holistic value* is only encouraged if it aligns with the agenda of the state, and *holistic value* not sanctioned by the state is usually suppressed. So, for example, in the former U.S.S.R. you would find diverse avenues of multidimensional nourishment encouraged and subsidized by the state, from investment in education and performing arts to reliable socialized healthcare. But freedom of speech and press were not encouraged, despite how enriching free expression of ideas is to human culture. Access to basic nutrition was ubiquitous, while the methods of food production, as devastating as they were to the environment because of the misuse of fertilizers and pesticides, could not be questioned or changed. We see similar contradictions in China, which, perhaps because of economic liberalization and the profit pressures it incites, has amplified many negative externalities over the past decade.

- In market-centric American style mixed economies within constitutional representative democracies, perverse valuations are actually the norm. *Holistic value* is pointedly discarded on the whole, and its recognition often aggressively lobbied against, because recognition of negative externalities interferes with profit - either because public awareness of them would potentially undermine consumer appeal, or because government awareness of such externalities can provoke costly regulation. Although increased consumer awareness is slowly shifting the Titanic with trends like green branding and sustainable sourcing, the mainstream business expectation still tends to be that delivering *holistic value* interferes with efficiencies, rather than becoming part of a definition of efficiency. Among certain demographics, *holistic value* prevails in purchasing decisions because those consumers have educated themselves about multidimensional risks and benefits. However, this increased awareness is restricted to a very small percentage of the overall population, a group with the interests, aptitudes, skills, time and means to counter a deluge of deceptively manipulative corporate marketing. As part of *holistic value*, the cultural capital inherent to "conscious consumerism" within that group usually plays a significant role. All of this results in boutique, high *holistic value* products that have a boutique, high exchange value. Meanwhile, the vast majority of consumers have only a vague idea that they are injuring themselves, their children and their environment through the consumption choices and habits advocated by commercialist corporationism.

- Among democratic mixed-economies with more central planning and less market-centric emphasis, *holistic value* tends to be recognized and even advocated, especially where elements of direct democracy or diverse and proportional parliamentary representation encourage multidimensional policy development. For example, the "precautionary principle" often championed in Germany and other European countries attempts to ensure thorough consideration of environmental externalities when deploying new products and technologies. The deceptive persuasion of certain kinds of advertising are also restricted with *holistic value* in mind; for example, direct consumer marketing of pharmaceuticals is not permitted in many of these countries. Also, because of the socialization of many essential services, the definition of efficiency or success is increasingly grounded in *holistic value*.

For example, in Great Britain, doctor pay in the socialized healthcare system has been tied directly to health outcomes of that doctor's patient population. In some countries, perverse valuations are further attenuated by the legalization and regulation of many things - such as recreational drugs - that are illegal in other countries (we'll discuss this topic more in a bit). All-in-all, the multidimensional awareness held by a small minority in the U.S. tends to be shared by a much larger percentage of the populace in these countries.

• In eco-centric models, the awareness to and adjustments for *holistic value* tend to be fairly well-developed, and in some cases quite extreme. To ride bikes everywhere, compost all kitchen waste, grow vegetables in a community garden, repair everything rather than buy new stuff, rely on alternative energy and perhaps even live entirely off the electrical grid - all of this provides a potent illusion that an eco-friendly footprint is being sustained. Unfortunately, most of these experiments are still embedded in mature market-centric economies, relying on the resources of the surrounding system to fill in where self-sufficiency cannot (medical intervention, library books, commercial clothing, videos from the Internet, etc.). As models for how human beings could live more sustainably and responsibly, these are encouraging examples, and indeed demonstrate that it is possible to prioritize *holistic value* in practical and effective ways. But they have seldom demonstrated a sustainability that is independent of the larger systems in which they reside.

I'll restrict the holistic valuation review to just these three approaches for now, since most of the others do not specifically address this issue, or assume some level of self-regulation regarding *holistic value* that either doesn't acknowledge the complexities of the modern age, or the deficiencies of commercialist corporationism.

When viewing political economies through the *property matrix* lens, what quickly becomes evident is that nearly all of them insist on controlling property through its position in the matrix. For example, even among anarchist ideals that reject authoritarian controls, *property position* is one of the persisting agreements without which anarchism could not function as proposed. How *property position* is enforced may vary among different anarchist proposals, and the institutions of enforcement may be more decentralized, but the fact is that some sort of force must of necessity be used to extend primary assumptions and preferences about property into a functional system, as well as to maintain that system over time. So regardless of what approach we take, and no matter how egalitarian or democratic our economic and political systems are, the mechanism of *property position* enforcement becomes central to its practicality and durability. Even if we advocate that all property should remain *common*, or that we should emphasize and celebrate property with a high *holistic value*, this assignment must persist in collective agreement, or it is just a fairy tale. So, once again, we arrive at that critical distinction between collective responsibility and individual freedom, for there will always be divergent opinions about where property should be located within the *property matrix*, either as the main focus of collective production or consumption, or as a privilege of individual accessibility or ownership.

In this way we come full circle back to moral creativity. What I am proposing is that how we view various forms of property, as well as how we enforce their position in the *property matrix*, directly correlates with the breadth of our moral imagination and the status of our moral development. This is true individually, in our interior conceptions of property and our emotional and volitional relationships with property, and collectively, in our values expressions in the structure of government and commerce, as political ideologies, and in the rule of law.   It seems obvious that, for any political economy, the ability to cohesively perpetuate advanced moral creativity and progressive moral development will be the foundation of its ongoing success.   To formulate and express a specific values hierarchy, and even temporarily influence sociopolitical outcomes with persuasion from that perspective, is an admirable feat. But it is not equivalent to sustaining that values hierarchy over multiple generations, or indeed over successive millennia of human civilization. For that, we require a widespread evolution in ethics that can easily replicate itself, and that is inherently resistant to both counterrevolution and cultural entropy.

A Process for Developing Design Criteria

In order to explore this question further, we need a moral compass for our journey. In Integral Lifework, that compass is a specific process bounded by a handful of assumptions. Those assumptions are as follows:

1. There is a predictable path of moral development.

2. There is a guiding intentionality that can reliably inspire, energize and focus moral creativity and moral development.

3. There are multidimensional nourishment practices that provide supportive structures for moral creativity and development, as well as opportunities to express and refine them.

4. There is a process that reliably guides multidimensional nourishment with wisdom and discernment, and provides metrics to evaluate the expressions of our moral creativity and development, so that necessary adjustments can be made.

As you can see, the process informs the assumptions which inform the process, so we won't be escaping the circular reasoning of moral creativity alluded to earlier. But that's okay, because we can still measure the outcomes and adjust our course. What remains then is to explain these assumptions and processes. Since I have written about them more extensively elsewhere, I will offer only the briefest of outlines here. To begin, what follow are some proposed strata of intuitive moral valuation. These are not really distinct stages through which we advance, but rather an architecture of interrelated orientations to ourselves and others that interact in a hierarchical fashion. These may express themselves at different times and in different ways within various dimensions of being - or within different contexts of interaction - but thoughts, feelings, actions and intuitions within a given stratum will always hint at both the presence of adjacent strata, and the possibility of forward (upward) movement. Which is to say that our individual or collective experience of a particular stratum will always suggest that there is a less sophisticated or more immature way to react or interact, and a more sophisticated and more mature way to react or interact, toward which we can, and perhaps must, advance. Our developmental orientation-of-the-moment will usually shift, fluidly and perpetually, based on our situational context, our cultural conditioning and our current level of health and wholeness in each of the twelve nourishment centers shortly to be defined.

Here, then, are those strata of intuitive moral valuation, starting with the equivalent of our biological infancy, and progressing from there. My thinking about this progression was initially inspired by Ken Wilber's research and observations in *Integral Psychology*. Recently, I was delighted to have these ideas reinforced by Lawrence Kohlberg's *Essays on Moral Development,* particularly in his discussions of *agape.* My insights have also been informed by ongoing work with clients and students, some formative mystical experiences, and the perpetual intersection of ideas from a wide range of sources, including many of the thinkers quoted earlier. Additional influences include Hāfez, Rumi, Sri Aurobindo, J. Krishnamurti, Jean Piaget, Jean Gebser, Tomas Merton, C.S. Lewis, Teilhard de Chardin, Freud, Jung, the Bhagavad Gita, the Christian Biblical canon and Nag Hammadi texts, the Dhammapada and Prajñāpāramitā, Plato and Lao Tzu. I also would add fiction writers like Dickens, Austen, Proust, Tolkein, Bradbury, Le Guinn, Steinbeck, Asimov and Philip K. Dick to the mix, as well as the many musicians, poets, painters, filmmakers and other artists who have injected memes into my consciousness over the years. And, like Marcus Aurelius, my own ethics and ideas about moral development have much to do with the friends, colleagues, mentors, lovers and family members who inspired me by example, nudging me onwards and upwards by love's design. Integrating all of these wonderful input streams has been as much a felt experience as an intellectual and spiritual one, mirroring the landscape of moral creativity itself.

- **Egoless Raw Need:** Naïve, helpless state in which volition is centered around unrestrained basic nourishment in every moment, but where the mechanisms of needs fulfillment are unknown, unskilled or otherwise inaccessible. In this stratum, the scope of one's "relevant timeframe" for this needs fulfillment is almost always the immediate, everpresent *now.*

- **Self-Assertive Egoism:** The aggressive utilization of basic tools to satisfy own wants and whims, usually without regard to the impact on others, is an overwhelming moral imperative here. In most situations, this imperative is only moderated by fear of "being caught" and the personal embarrassment, punishment or loss of personal nourishment that may follow.   The relevant timeframe for fulfilling one's desires expands a little here, so that gratification can be delayed until the near-future. However, the past is largely irrelevant, except as a reminder of negative consequences to be avoided.

- **Self-Protective Egoism:** Moral function is governed by acquisitive, manipulative, consumptive or hedonistic patterns that accumulate and defend personal gains (i.e. secure nourishment sources) in order to insulate the ego from risks and loss. This self-centeredness may be masked by primitive adaptive personas that navigate basic reciprocity, but is generally indifferent to other people except for the ability of others to satisfy personal demands. Now the past can actually become more important than the present, because the past is where wrongs were suffered and gains realized. Reflections on the present and future, on the other hand, tend to be inhabited by fear of risk and loss.

- **Tribal Acceptance:**   Conformance with social expectations, and approval of one's primary social group(s), governs moral function here.   What is "right" or "wrong" is defined by what increases or attenuates social capital and standing within the group(s). The acknowledged link between personal survival and tribal acceptance expands self-centeredness to tribe-centeredness, but otherwise operates similarly to lower moral strata. In this stratum, one's "tribe" tends to be fairly immediate, and fairly small - a family, team, group of peers, gang, etc. Now the relevant timeframe shifts back into the immediate future, where status and influence will either be lost or realized; the past may still be instructive, but what waits around the next bend in the road is what preoccupies.

- **Defensive Tribalism:** Here the social order and internal rules of our primary social group(s) are championed as correct and proper both within the tribe (regulation) and to the outside world (proselytization). Competition with - and subjugation of - other individuals or groups outside of the tribe (or one's class, caste or social position) becomes more pronounced. Thus moral function is defined by rigid definitions and legalistic rules (law & order, right & wrong, black & white) that justify and secure personal standing within the tribe, as well as the tribe's standing within a given environment. Now, because one's tribal position is secure, the past again dominates. Past authorities, traditions, insights and experiences infuse the present legalistic frame with self-righteous justification.

- **Opportunistic Individualism:** This stratum is part of an individuation process from the tribe and the tribe's values hierarchy. Moral orientation may lapse into previous strata, but is otherwise centered around a sense of obligation to one's own uniqueness, freedom, well-being and wholeness. As a result, one is open to more complex nourishment that was not available within egoic or tribal orientations. Probably as a component of emancipation from tribal expectations, there tends to be minimal concern about the impact of one's individuation process on others. In this stratum, the present once again gains preeminence; the past is being left behind, and the future matters less than assertiveness in the now.

- **Contributive Individualism:** Now more fully individuated from the primary tribe and its social constraints, one continues to be committed to one's own well-being, freedom, wholeness and access to more subtle, nuanced and complex nourishment resources. Moral function is increasingly defined by efforts that appear "good" or helpful to others, as framed by conscience, the context-of-the-moment and one-on-one relationships. In this sense, moral relativism is derived from one's own experiences and interactions, and tends to be maintained and defended within this self-referential absorption. The present is still paramount here.

- **Competitive Communalism:** Moral function is strongly influenced by personal acceptance of the importance of participating in a mutually beneficial and lawfully just community, while still retaining individual uniqueness. However, this initial expansion into a communal moral orientation usually orbits around competition. Competition with others for personal positional power and influence in the community; competition with other moral orientations, asserting the relevance of one's own views and priorities; non-conformance with, and continual challenging of, a community's established values hierarchy; and competition for various forms of social capital. In this stratum the future gains more importance as one strategizes navigation of these competitions. The past also regains its teaching role, with emphasis on both failures and successes to inform current strategies.

- **Cooperative Communalism:** Here a communal role and collective responsibility is firmly accepted and established as part of moral function, and community is defined by shared values and experiences, rather than just shared benefits or just laws. The necessity of collaborative contribution to human welfare is understood, and the desire to compete for personal advantage fades away. A community's shared values are appreciated, integrated and supported in order to further that community's goals and collective nourishment, but without the suppression or sacrificing of personal values and identity that were common in earlier tribalism. Thus distinctions of class, caste, and social position tend to attenuate. This stratum tends to invite preoccupation with the future, sometimes even beyond one's personal future, because one is charting a course through increased complexity. Time is experienced and conceived as episodic.

- **Principled Rationalism:** Moral function is now defined by a rationally defined set of reasoned moral principles, principles with the unifying objective of benefiting all of humanity. For anyone operating in this stratum, empirical validation of moral efficacy is of particularly compelling interest; what really works should be embraced, and what doesn't should be discarded. There is also an additional form of individuation here, where identification with previous communities (communities whose values and goals had previously been facilitated and integrated) begins to fade, and is replaced with increasing identification with, and compassion for, all human beings. Social divisions are discarded in favor of equal status. The future can now become an all-consuming fixation that drives more and more decisions, the past becomes an advising reference, and the current moment a fleeting absorption. As a result, time tends to both constrict and accelerate in this stratum, remaining linear in experience and conception.

- **World-Centric:** Now there is a greater appreciation and acceptance of ecologies that facilitate, transcend and include human society. These ecologies may contain biological, metaphysical, quantum or other systems-oriented constructs, with the feature that these systems are vast, complex and interdependent. Here moral function is inspired by individual and collective commitment to understanding and supporting those systems in order to support all life. Personal identification with this broader, ecological consciousness expands humanity-centric compassion and concern into world-centric compassion and concern. Values hierarchies now begin to be viewed as a primary form of nourishment, from which all other nourishment is derived. Time dilates and slows a bit here, tending to be viewed more as cycles and patterns than a line.

• **Transpersonal Holism:** This stratum is marked by an increasing flexibility of moral orientation. For example, the realization that more than one values hierarchy can be valid, that someone can operate within multiple values hierarchies simultaneously, or that seemingly opposing values hierarchies can synthesize a new, higher order moral orientation. This intersubjective moral ambiguity is then navigated through the discernment of intentional, strategic outcomes that benefit the largest majority possible. Definition of what constitutes "the largest majority possible" likewise changes and evolves, but is strongly informed by transpersonal perceptions and experiences. In turn, identification with this transpersonal connectedness subordinates other identifications, so that, for example, experiencing a shared ground of being is indistinguishable from compassionate affection for all beings, and compassionate affection for all beings is indistinguishable from attenuation of individual ego. The relevant timeframe for this stratum becomes contextual; the relevance of past, present and future shifts with current priorities, and the cycles and patterns of time begin to give way to a continuum.

- **Spiritual Universality:**   Through persistent and intimate connection with an absolute, universal inclusiveness of being, moral function is defined by whatever most skillfully facilitates "the good of All." "The good of All," in turned, is an evolving intuition, a successive unfolding of mystical awareness in concert with dialectical cognition and neutrality of personal will. However, it tends to remain more of a felt sense than an exclusively rational construct. Skillfulness can still be refined through empirical experimentation and observation, but it is always subjected to a filter of intensified and unconditional compassion - a felt sense as well. Identification with the All is fluid and seamless, and moral thought and action flowing from this identification are also fluid and seamless. That is not to say that this stratum can't occasionally be interrupted by regressions to previous strata within one or more dimensions of being (usually as a reaction to overwhelming or stressful situations), but the contrast and incongruity of those regressions is strikingly obvious. Past, present and future become a continuum where "now" is less fixed; the experience of time itself is more relative and process-oriented.   Nevertheless, "now" remains the primary reference for that process.

- **Applied Nonduality:**   This is an expression of mystical, nondual consciousness as a supremely unfettered existence where intuitions of universal freedom are fully realized. There is a certain irony that the autonomy one's ego so craved in earlier strata is now readily available through the absence of ego. The lack of a distinct sense of self in some ways eradicates any sort of identification at all - so non-being is equivalent to being, and self is equivalent to both nothingness and previous conceptions of "the All."   Here   inexhaustible   loving   kindness   is conclusively harmonized through advanced forms of

discernment.   An   enduring   all-inclusive   love-
consciousness   integrates   all   previous   moral
orientations, current intentions and actions into a
carefree - but nevertheless carefully balanced - flow;
a flow into what might be described as "ultimate
purpose." Previous orientations are then viewed not
as right or wrong, but as a spectrum of imperfect
expressions of that ultimate purpose. In this final
letting go of self-identification, all nourishment is
love, all love is nourishment, and all values
hierarchies   are   subordinated   to   skillfully
compassionate affection.   At the same time, this
realization and any other constructs become just
that: constructs, inventions of the mind. Up until
now, the main concern of moral valuation has been
the orientation of self-to-self, self-to-other, self-to-
community, self-to-environment, self-to-planet, self-
to-humanity, self-to-nothingness, self-to-All, etc. In
other words, previous values hierarchies tended to be
preoccupied with the context of the self. In this
stratum, that context is no longer relevant, because
there is no self, and no concept of no-self. Along the
same lines, the past/present/future construction of
time dissolves into insignificance.

In discussing any such progression, questions inevitably
arise as to whether all of these are sequential or mandatory
steps in a moral maturation process, whether each stratum
represents a permanent transformation or merely presents
additional menu options for moral valuation, whether all
dimensions of being (individually or collectively) advance at
the same rate through these strata, whether the strata are
memes that can be transmitted and replicated across
human populations, whether they are just a priori
assumptions or can be empirically validated...and so on.
The short answer is that these strata of moral valuation are
a continuum of responses to the question of self-
contextualization, and consequently influence identity

formation over time. This influence can be personal or collective, either an individual, self-transformative impulse, or a shared societal movement. I also think the means of propagation can be memetic, either superficially through mass media, or more structurally and enduringly through interpersonal relationship.

As a continuum, however, any proposed compart-mentalization or stratification will always be fairly arbitrary and subjective, influenced more by available language and the concepts inhabiting various disciplines (psychology, anthropology, spirituality, philosophy, etc.) than empirically observable demarcations. Nevertheless, once such divisions are established, we can begin to chart how human self-concept, interrelationship, motivation, and values hierarchies are expressed from one individual or group to the next, and how these expressions relate to moral functions across such defined strata. These observations can't validate particular divisions of the continuum, but they do just suggest a way to organize human behavior - and indeed a way to organize our approach to civil society and its institutions. Furthermore, these expressions will be different from one dimension of being to the next, from one individual to the next, from one culture or subculture to the next, from one historical context to the next, and even from one moment to the next in each of these situations. It is extremely difficult to predict how these layers will manifest...only that, as a general hint of forward movement, they do manifest in measurable ways.

Are they dependent in a hierarchical sense? They are certainly interdependent, and do insinuate a preferential hierarchy into moral function, but the particular sequence of apprehension, integration and expression seems to me as diverse and multifaceted as human personality and culture itself. Momentary insights are available in any stratum from any other, to be sure, and one or more dimensions of being may advance more quickly than others, while one or more dimensions may actually regress. This is another reason why holistic, multidimensional nourishment is so important. Regardless, however, moral function does not appear to be static, permanent, or perfect, and neither is its evolution.

How then do these moral valuations relate to the question of personal freedom and collective responsibility? First, let's consider what lies at the zenith of this particular progression: "an enduring all-encompassing love-consciousness" that integrates, well, everything into an ultimate purpose. If we are to invite less developed strata into higher elevations, the key will be to demonstrate this unitive zenith in both our formulations of political economy and the types of exchanges that political economy promotes, in every interpersonal exchange in which we engage, and everywhere in between. But how is that possible? How can we embody this transformative, all-encompassing love-consciousness? And how can we do it skillfully and effectively? In Integral Lifework, the starting point for all such transformation is our interior multidimensionality - the twelve dimensions we seek to nourish and harmonize into wholeness. Once that interior work begins, it can gradually be projected outward, across multiple domains of exchange - across ever-enlarging arenas of intention and action. Without the stable, supportive structures of fully nourished interior dimensions, projection into other arenas will not be consistent or reliable, and is likely to become self-depleting, self-defeating or otherwise unsustainable. This has been my observation at the interpersonal, small group, organizational and community levels, but it is only my tentative hypothesis that, at larger scales, the fractal pattern holds.

What are these twelve dimensions, then? Here is a brief overview of the twelve, sketched on a personal scale:

- **Healthy Body.** Sustaining and strengthening our physical being through conscious patterns of diet, exercise, sleep and other key factors uniquely suited to who we are. What this looks like will vary from person to person, but one key component is listening to our own body's promptings to know what is really the most nourishing.

- **Playful Heart.** Maintaining healthy emotional expression and connection with our inner life, and engaging in regular playfulness and creative self-expression from day to day. Once again each person will benefit from different avenues of play and creativity, and once again we must learn how to listen to our own heart's joys and longings, and be guided by them here.

- **Supportive Community.** Inviting love and acceptance into our lives, both in what we receive from others, how loving and accepting we are of others, and how actively we participate in our community. This will also look different for each person – and for the same person over the course of their life.

- **Expanding Mind.** Building, broadening and routinely stimulating our knowledge, understanding and mental capacities and abilities. For one person this may mean regularly researching new topics of interest; for another it may mean having spirited discussions with friends; for another this nourishment may take the form of watching plays or films that challenge their perspective, or reading books that stretch their imagination; for another this may mean playing chess. It will be different for everyone, with the shared result of sharpening and strengthening mental faculties.

- **Fulfilling Purpose.** Discovering and actuating a satisfying life-purpose that is perfectly matched to our authentic self, and which supports the focus, strength and healthy expression of our personal will. This may be a lifelong pursuit, expressing itself in many stages and transitions, but the fundamental act of exploring activities and interests that resonate with our essence – that strongly persuade us of what is most meaningful to us by inspiring and energizing our efforts – is the core nourishment practice here.

- **Authentic Spirit.** Establishing and increasing our connection and interaction with the ground of being – described in different traditions as the fundamental essence, spiritual energy, potential for liberation, or divine nature of reality – and translating that deepening connection into a spiritually authentic life. This, too, will be different for each person, and may require years of exploration and experimentation with different spiritual disciplines to fully appreciate and understand. This does not mean, however, that we need to become religious or subscribe to some established belief system, just that we explore and sustain this dimension of being. As with all other dimensions, there are suggestions for how we can achieve this within Integral Lifework, but each person must find their own way.

- **Restorative History.** Acknowledging, honoring and, when necessary, reprocessing all the experiences of our lives – whether remembered or forgotten, integrated or rejected – that have contributed to our current state of being; every significant relationship, trauma, milestone, accomplishment, perception or influence that has led us to the present moment. There are specific practices suggested within Integral Lifework to accomplish this, but once again how this dimension is nourished will be different for each person. For some this may require heart-to-heart conversations with family members. For others this may mean reviewing life experiences and how they have shaped self-concept. And for others this dimension may be so traumatic or confusing that it requires the assistance of professional therapy. But, like all the others, it is essential to wholeness and well-being.

- **Pleasurable Legacy.** Creating and sustaining new life, pleasurable experiences that are shared, and an enduring and positive impression on our world, while at the same time maintaining a sense of safety and stability for ourselves and those we love. For many people this dimension is all about creating a home and having children – who in turn are encouraged in turn to create a home and have children of their own. But there are many other ways this dimension can be effectively nourished. For one person this may entail writing novels. For another this may involve a lifetime of community service. For someone else this may mean being an educator, or establishing some sort of business or nonprofit organization, or perhaps inventing some kind of helpful technology. But all of these avenues share the characteristics of both being pleasurable for the individual, and sharing that pleasure beyond one's own lifespan. The synthesis of pleasure and legacy is nourishment for this dimension.

- **Flexible Processing Space.** This means being able to regularly and effortlessly transition through different modes of processing, with each centered in different facets of our being – the heart, mind, body, spirit and soul – so that we fully nourish those facets and create transparent access to the insights, wisdom and discernment each has to offer. In part, this is learned through nourishing all the other dimensions of being. But there are also specific practices (including mental, emotional, physical and spiritual disciplines within Integral Lifework) that encourage in-depth exposure to each type of processing, and a means of effortless transitioning between them.

- **Empowered Self-Concept.** This dimension is about understanding what we think about ourselves, how we feel about ourselves, and how we arrived at those conclusions. Here we expand our self-awareness, explore our self-worth, and define what it means to live our lives effectively – that is, to achieve what we set out to achieve and successfully navigate the complex world around us. So nourishment in this dimension is as much about looking inward as it is about looking outward at the consequences of our actions; it equally emphasizes how we subjectively perceive ourselves, and how we can concretely measure our effectiveness in the mysterious task of living.

- **Satisfying Sexuality.** Here we explore the nature of our own sexuality. What does sexual gratification feel like for us? What does intimacy look like to us? How do sexuality and intimacy intersect for us? How do sexuality and intimacy express themselves in our relationships? Answers to these questions will vary for each person, so nourishment will look different for each person as well – and it will inevitably change over time. But the more clearly we can answer these questions, the more effectively we can nurture this dimension.

- **Affirming Integrity.** This involves consciously aligning the unfolding essence of our being with our thoughts, feelings, words and actions, so that how we are from moment to moment authentically reflects who we are in our innermost depths.

What do these dimensions represent? They are an organic structure of self-care categories as observed in my work with Integral Lifework clients, mysticism students, employees I have managed, and people I have counseled in various capacities over the past thirty years. From these conceptual placeholders, I have worked backwards to discern the building blocks of each nourishment center, identifying four primary drives (to *exist*, *experience*, *adapt* and *affect*, as expressions of being), and sixteen fulfillment impulses that satisfy primary drives in different contexts. Fulfillment impulses include things like autonomy, discovery, mastery, avoidance, belonging, imagination, effectiveness and so on (a complete list is provided at the end of this book). All that really concerns us here, however, are the twelve nourishment dimensions, because political economy of any scale must address them; it must, in some way, balance the individual freedom to engage in all of these dimensions, as openly and expansively as possible, with the collective responsibilities necessary to ensure that all nourishment components, opportunities and resources are available to everyone.

To recap, the cycle looks like this: the "fulfillment orientation" of transformative, all-encompassing love-consciousness energizes twelve dimensions of being, which in turn provide supportive structures to sustain and expand transformative, all-encompassing love-consciousness. Through this repeating cycle, then engine of transformation is engaged within ourselves, then our relationships, our workplace, our community, our city, interactions with our natural environment and so on. Below is a diagram excerpted from *True Love* that encompasses some of the concepts discussed so far.

Diagram: *Transformative Engine*

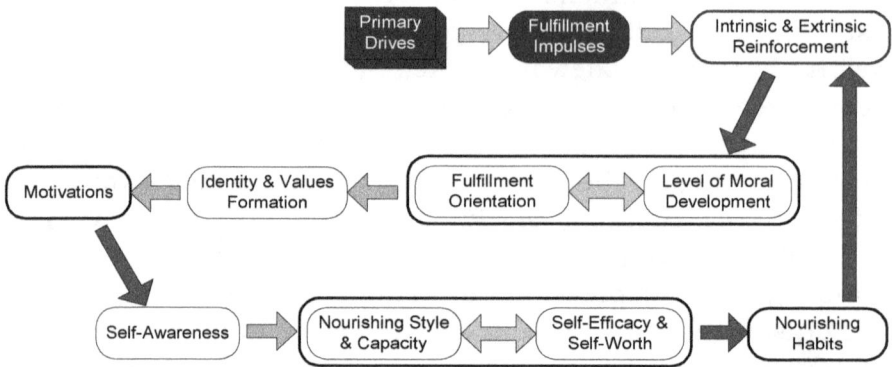

Clearly, whatever strata of moral valuation the majority of our twelve dimensions happen to be functioning within will either enhance or impede this cycle. But another advantage of multidimensional nourishment is that it also stimulates our moral development and creativity. To be clear, multidimensional nourishment involves balanced engagement with all of these dimensions, rather obsession with any one of them. Because of our native strengths and weaknesses, careful attention is required to overcome barriers to nurturing in some areas, or overindulgence and excessive reliance in others, in a conscious effort to synergize a whole. In any case, this journey towards wholeness goads us, gently but firmly, in the direction of all-encompassing love-consciousness, with its gradual unfolding and precedence of evolving values hierarchies. Our capacity for moral creativity is indeed innate, but it must be nurtured. And this is really how we arrive at the *unitive principle*, for as we nourish and integrate all dimensions, one unitive impulse is being expressed in an interior harmonization; and as our morality evolves, our relationships with others, with Nature, and indeed with the Universe itself also embodies the same unitive orientation. As within, so without. We may still differentiate, but it is for the sake of an all-inclusive unity that flows forth from love-consciousness.

Why is this so? As Plotinus asks in the *Enneads*:

> "No doubt strength and grace of form go well enough with the idea of rarefied body; but what can this rarefied body want with moral excellence? On the contrary its interest would lie in being comfortable in its environments and contacts, in being warmed or pleasantly cool, in bringing everything smooth and caressing and soft around it: what could it care about a just distribution?"

Is it the natural maturation of a more sophisticated and far-seeing self-interest that inspires a unitive vision? Is it an inevitable evolutionary refinement in social relations? Is it an arbitrary hiccup in the development of the brain that provides some adaptive advantage? Is it evidence of a divine imprint on the human psyche, or part of what Sri Aurobindo called "supramentalisation," the ongoing descent of the divine into the material plane? I have my suspicions, but of course I don't know the answer. I have just observed it over and over again: the *unitive principle* appears to be firmly embedded in holistic nourishment and moral creativity as a function of natural maturation and growth, with continuously humanizing, harmonizing and liberating effects. And this why I believe transformative, all-encompassing love-consciousness should become our guiding intentionality for everything, including models of political economy, because this kind of skillfully compassionate affection has proven itself to be the most constructive force available to us.

How do we learn about this *unitive principle*?   I think turning to the our "inner Light," as so many others have done before, is an excellent starting point; that is what many Integral Lifework practices are about.   In Aristotle's language, we could say that balanced, harmonious, multidimensional nourishment (i.e. "intermediate" nourishment that is not excessive or defective in any dimension) leads to virtuous actions and character, a reciprocation that in turn amplifies both moral sophistication and capacity.   There is also the rich availability of wisdom traditions we have touched upon to support that journey.   And there is, hopefully, the moral training provided us - albeit selectively - by our closest relationships.

> [When I recently reread the opening pages of *The Thoughts of Marcus Aurelius*, where he describes in detail all that he learned from beloved family members, friends and mentors, I could not help but weep. It is of course a testimony to the quality of his character that the Emperor so lovingly attributes that character to the tutelage and examples of others. But what moved me more than that, as reinforced my own experience, is how exceedingly rare those inspiring relationships are, and how, as Marcus Aurelius gently and respectfully captures, in the course of life events we must say farewell to them all. I think that, the older I get, the more precious, and potent, the musings of that old Roman become.]

Our final assumption concerns the nuts and bolts of decision-making, especially in the context of designing and evaluating proposed models.   In Integral Lifework, it is impossible to achieve any sort of wisdom or discernment without accessing and integrating both the information unique to multiple dimensions of being, and exercising the processing style of each dimension, which is equally unique. This is really the heart of the Flexible Processing

Space dimension. As J.L. Mackie wrote in *Ethics: Inventing Right and Wrong*: "If we were aware of [objective values], it would have to be by some special faculty of moral perception or intuition, utterly different from out ordinary ways of knowing everything else." And there are, in fact, any number of long-practiced techniques, found mainly among mystical wisdom traditions, to invite such a "special faculty," but I won't focus on those at this time. Instead, I'll touch on some of the principle features of those techniques. For one, we would always want cultivate a guiding intentionality for our practice: a genuine desire for the good of All. For example, using a mantra like "May Love and Light arise in All that Is, and All that Is arise in Love and Light" to set our intention. Then, as we maintain that orientation, we relax our personal ego and willfulness, generating an inner neutrality that allows multiple input streams to sit lightly in our consciousness...just sitting, relaxing, letting go, and settling in. In this way, Aristotle might say that we are "finding the middle of the circle."

Essentially, what we are trying to do is relinquish habits or patterns that reinforce any one mode of being as a primary processing space, and instead cultivate a neutral interior environment that is open to input from multiple perspectives. Those perspectives actually originate from different centers of intelligence, including somatic intelligence, emotional intelligence, analytical intelligence, spiritual intelligence and so forth. This openness has very specific qualities, in that personal volition is deliberately suspended in all respects, except for a condition of subtle, inviting neutrality. We could call this a method of interior consensus, or intuitive synthesis, or aperspectival integration, or aggregation-in-emptiness, or we could invent any number of other descriptions using specialized language from different disciplines. All of these are fingers pointing to the moon, of course, but they provide some broad brush strokes for skillful discernment through inclusive receptivity and engagement. The result, in this context, is what constitutes "wisdom."

[On an individual level, this neutral integration process is achieved through techniques of self-awareness in each dimension, unified through structured and unstructured practices that shift our perception-cognition into different modes - these are outlined in many of the exercises found in the Integral Lifework books. On a collective level, this same process can be embodied in participatory synergies, where intersubjective synthesis is encouraged in open, honest and compassionate communication and group practice. There are some proven guidelines for how to engineer this neutral openness in various contexts, and I cover one of these in an introductory way in the Integral Coregroups section of *Being Well*. The model presented there is mainly about creating a mutually supportive environment for holistic nourishment, but much of it translates quite easily into facilitating other objectives, such as practicing neutral awareness. What I have concluded after years of experimentation and observation is that the ideal size of such groups is between eight and twelve people, and that in any group larger than that the quality and inclusivity of synthesis begins to break down.]

Including multiple perspectives in a decision-making process isn't all that new, of course. Interdisciplinary partnerships and information sharing are a proven advantage in an increasingly complex world. All that we are doing here is identifying some dimensions for consideration. As a superficial but still instructive example, we can correlate each nourishment center with a specific project in order to demonstrate the process. Let's say a group is trying to make a decision about the best types of energy to build or acquire for powering their community. Here is how a handful of dimensions correlate to multiple input streams to formulate design criteria:

- **Healthy Body.** What are the advantages and disadvantages of this solution with regard to physical health and well-being, both in the community and as projected into wider arenas of concern (natural environment, etc.)?

- **Playful Heart.** Is there a way to include creative expression into this energy system? To beautify the technology? Or somehow integrate the solution with existing creative facilities and activities in the community?

- **Supportive Community.** How does this solution impact neighboring communities or the regional power system? How will the community be engaged in its implementation, utilization and maintenance? How will mutual benefit and buy-in ensure a successful rollout?

- **Expanding Mind.** Is this solution truly innovative? Is it within the capacities of the community's training and experience resources to manage and maintain? Does it encourage intellectual resourcefulness, or somehow deplete it?

- **Fulfilling Purpose.** Does this facilitate the collectively agreed-upon purpose and direction of the community as whole?

- **Restorative History.** Does this solution correct mistakes in energy production, distribution and use that were made in the past, or inadvertently repeat them in a new form?

- **Pleasurable Legacy.** What legacy will this investment provide future generations, both within the community and as an example for other communities?

- **Empowered Self-Concept.** Does this approach model community self-reliance? Does it enhance community self-esteem? Do the planning, implementation and ongoing maintenance provide improved levels of self-awareness for the community?

- **Affirming Integrity.** Does the energy generation and distribution process align with the expressed values, and values hierarchies, of the community? For example, will it be managed through a democratic process? Is it ecologically sustainable? Does it serve everyone equally?

These are just sketches of a multidimensional approach, but it provides a sense of what is involved. If love-consciousness is inherent to the process, and moral function is sufficiently advanced, these considerations will tend to be reflexive. Otherwise, they can be introduced and modeled by skillfully compassionate mentors, activists, community leaders and small group facilitators. But what is happening here is a reinforcement of moral function in the planning, decision-making and implementation process. Over time, through endless iterations of multidimensional nourishment across limitless contextual variations, the moral maturation process takes root and wont let go. Yes, all of this is also dependent on every individual's effort to sustain balanced, holistic nurturing of themselves, but the participatory application of the same nourishment commitment will - inexplicably but inevitably, I believe - galvanize collective growth and transformation in a parallel fashion.

How Property Position, Moral Creativity and Multidimensional Nourishment Define the Evolution of Political Economy

And now, at long last, we arrive at the intersection of *property position,* moral creativity and multidimensional nourishment. Here is what undergirds our central hypothesis: the further along we are in our moral development, the more we will assign property to progressively inclusive categories that promote an equally shared benefit for all. What is happening here, I believe, is simply the *unitive principle* applying itself to *property position.* This principle holds for both individual and collective assignment (or the implicit collective agreement on *property position,* as it were), and so some of my language here reflects that. Here's what that progression looks like for the *ownership* and *holistic value* axes, after consolidating some of the strata described early into more convenient Levels of moral function:

> **Level 1**. In Egoless Raw Need, property *ownership* categorization hasn't yet occurred. In a strange sense, all property is probably viewed as *common* and boundryless; it is a limitless resource existing only to

service to fundamental appetites and willful imperatives. There is not yet a care for, or conception of, *ownership* assignment or exclusion. In the same way, *holistic value* is monodimensional: there is only the primary and singular raw need that subjugates all nourishment differentiation.

Level 2. In the Egoic valuation strata, an I/Me/Mine moral orientation organizes property into the most *private*, personally consolidated state possible. Anything that hasn't yet been acquired is viewed as *potential* property, and nothing is *sacred*. Likewise, *holistic value* is generated through I/Me/Mine calculations, and there is only a vague sense of nourishment differentiation, usually derived from the current and most compelling appetite.

Level 3. As moral function evolves through Tribal strata, a more *communal* categorization may take hold for a few shared resources, but the emphasis will still remain on extensive privatization and various hierarchies of *private* property. Even from a Tribal perspective, "communal" may just represent a form of elitist privatization for the most influential class, and so here, too, anything not yet privatized will be viewed as *potential* in nature, including *wild things*. *Public domain* property is only grudgingly tolerated in order to facilitate and secure an exchange economy for *private* property. *Sacred* property may be defined in these strata, but only for the prestige or perceived advantage of the tribe in competition with other tribes. Now externals begin influencing *holistic value* formation, as the tribe's priorities usurp personal gratification. However, *holistic valuation* remains fairly abstracted from *exchange values*.

Level 4. In Individualistic moral orientations, *communal* property becomes increasingly employed for the collective benefit of affinitive or opportunistic associations, and we might even see the first glimpses of *public domain* allocation beyond the facilitation of secure exchange, if only to be perceived as concerned about the collective good. However, even such *public domain* assignments will be tentative; in reality everything in the *public domain* is still *potential* property, only temporarily or conditionally set aside. So *private* property still maintains its principal importance in these strata, if sometimes dressed up for the constructive illusion of collective advantage. Assignments of *sacred* property are also tolerated for the same reason, but *wild things* are still viewed as *common* or *potential* property. *Holistic value* can now be calculated more flexibly, with a perceived advantage-of-the-moment in mind, along with all previous input streams. Nourishment differentiation is more defined, but its interdependence is not yet appreciated, and so negative externalities are generally dismissed. Thus *holistic valuation* still has little correlation with *exchange value.*

Level 5. As Individualistic imperatives wane, a more Communal flavor of property assignment takes hold. Initially, there will be a desire to maintain *private* property for personal gain, but eventually that privatization is understood to be collectively shared by an exclusive group, and collective advantage begins to outweigh personal advantage. Tentative *public domain* property is still assigned because of its exchange facility within the community and with other communities, but it retains its *potential* to become *communal* property, especially if other, highly valued resources become depleted. In these strata anything not perceived as having such *potential* may be relegated to *common* or *sacred* property, once again increasing prestige for the community, but this orientation is eventually held with less exclusivity, and a more generous attitude of access and benefit to other communities. A fuller understanding of interdependent nourishment processes leads to a broader, more inclusive calculation of *holistic value*. Positive and negative externalities now gain importance in that calculation as well, especially when they impact social and cultural capital within and between communities. Thus *holistic value* begins to influence *exchange value* to a greater degree.

Level 6. Arriving at the stratum of Principled Rationalism, the property organization of previous Tribal, Individual and Communal moral orientation is more vigorously challenged. *Public domain* property now becomes the ideal categorization, with *private* and *communal* assignments subordinated to that objective. For the first time, setting aside *wild things* as *sacred* may be considered, but mainly as an investment for future resource depletion or other *public domain* need; so, provisionally *sacred* until a scarcity crisis assigns it to *potential*. The desire to maintain an egalitarian *public domain* property categorization can, however, lead to behaviors that echo previous moral orientations; for example, a de facto elitist privatization of property "held in public trust" but controlled mainly by the most influential class, for the benefit of that class. *Holistic value* calculations now have a much more diverse and inclusive basis, as collective understanding of what constitutes nourishment and the interdependence of all nourishment dimensions becomes more sophisticated. *Exchange value* is increasingly aligned with this more complex *holistic value* across most OSI *abstraction* layers.

Level 7. In the World-Centric moral valuation stratum, all previous property categorizations dissolve into a dominant *common* property paradigm. Because of a now firmly established interdependent systems orientation, any designations of *private*, *potential* and *communal* property become increasingly non-existent. Even *public domain* property becomes a temporary holding space for transition to *common* property assignment. We also see an enlarging scope of *wild things* set aside as perpetually *sacred*, not as an investment for future utility, but because *wild things* are esteemed in and of themselves (i.e. have intrinsic value independent of human valuation). Once the commonization of property is pervasive, there is no longer an elite class to disrupt or exclude others from sharing equally in property benefits. And because there is so little *private* property, a conventional exchange economy no longer exists in the mainstream. However, until commonization is complete, other property categorizations and their resultant economies and classes can persist, creating an organic, hybrid environment that is understandably tumultuous and unstable, but nevertheless reaches onward towards Level 8. At this stage, a subtle, multidimensional and highly sophisticated *holistic valuation* is replacing *exchange value* in human relationships with property across all OSI *abstraction* layers.

Level 8. In Transpersonal Holism, the process of commonization is now complete. There may still be pockets within the commonized architecture that hold on to previous property categorizations, but they become exceptions that are functionally and systemically isolated within the accepted status quo. Because of the intersubjective validation promoted in this stratum, systems and institutions are resilient enough to tolerate a broad diversity of moral function while still advancing a higher order moral orientation, thus the tumult we saw in a World-Centric stratum subsides. Through this stabilization, many forms of what in previous strata were considered to be *potential* property can now effortlessly be designated as *sacred*, purely to honor and celebrate their intrinsic value. In this level, the concepts of exclusion or exclusivity are so rare that even the designation of *personal* property becomes unnecessary. Thus even the concept of *holistic value* itself no longer provides significant differentiation from internalized values hierarchies or collective relationships with property. All the multiplicities of nourishment have now been integrated into a single thought field - an integral noosphere - so that *holistic value* becomes a collective experience and intuitive understanding that validates itself.

Level 9. Spiritual Universality begins to revise the *common* property designation still further. The desire to elevate intersubjectivity relaxes until a more unitive perspective permeates all valuations. Now there is a shared intuition that everything that once resided in other *ownership* categories is actually *sacred*. In fact, those previous categorizations are mainly perceived as destructive and unhealthy, and so any lingering subordinate relationships with property dissolve. However, because this stratum is so fluid - and because it can still be interrupted by regression - subordinate relationships may appear and disappear as required in continuously revising contexts. Despite these difficult but sometimes necessary hiccups, the primary flow of Level 9 is that the entirety of existence has intrinsic value, and so all human activity must engage that existence with unconditional compassion. There is also a strong intuition of a shared, unifying purpose, and an increasing desire to acquiesce into that purpose. At this stage, *holistic value* becomes equivalent to the *sacred*, intrinsic value that is collectively held.

Level 10.   In Applied Nonduality, the concept of property and its categorizations, valuations and layers of abstraction evaporates entirely, and regression to into previous moral orientations is barely conceivable. The unending flow of an actualized, overarching purpose is all that remains here, as guided and energized by an all-inclusive love-consciousness.

Diagram: Unitive Property Positioning

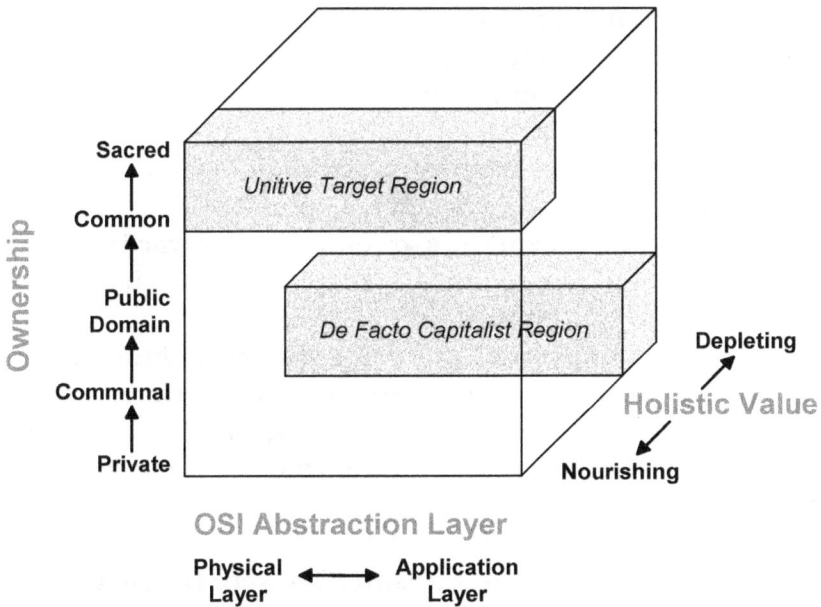

Where the previous descriptions of advancing moral sophistication were about relating self-to-other, the progression described here concerns the relating of self-to-property.   As with self-to-other relationships, self-to-property relationships also become more and more inclusive until dynamic unity is achieved; thus we can perceive a *unitive principle* for both types of relationship.   Is there an empirical means of testing the accuracy of such correlations? There may be, but right now this is mainly a grand hypothesis derived from observations, mystical practices, the writings of philosophers, and the teachings of a broad spectrum of spiritual traditions.   Among my observations of relationships (in everything from managing employees to mediating disputes to counseling couples), shared values identification, along with an awareness of different perceptions or perspectives around common experiences, leads to greater empathy, mutual compassion and understanding.   The predictable expansion of self-identity to include others (or at least certain aspects of others) in these contexts inherently produces greater information and resource sharing;   it is an almost automatic consequence of a reconciliation and interpersonal investment process.   In mystical practice - that is, the routine and disciplined activation of mystical perception-cognition - unitive insights and a gradual letting go of egoic selfhood routinely reinforce these same compassionate and generous orientations towards others. And so it should come as no surprise that, among the world's greatest spiritual traditions, the reliable demonstration of spiritual maturity always includes letting go of willful selfishness, a greater commitment to helping others, a collectivizing of resources, and a resolute departure from acquisitive patterns of thought and behavior.

The OSI layers of functional *abstraction* were barely touched upon here, mainly because each function has less to do with moral evolution, and more to do with technological advancement.   It seems probable, however, that if technology advances along with morality, the *unitive principle* will be reflected here as well.   That is, the OSI layers themselves will begin to integrate and merge, until there is less and less differentiation between the most abstract and intangible, and the most tangible and concrete. We can imagine a distant future in which the human mind, body, heart and spirit no longer perceives itself as separate from either Nature or humanly created things; where we are unified with existence, and all of existence is unified with itself, so that we are no longer acting upon that existence, but as part of its energy and flow.

Can we apply the *unitive principle* to political systems and institutions? I think we can, simply by observing how different political approaches organize decision-making authority according to the same levels of moral function. We can even rely on the same *ownership* categorizations and *holistic value* calculations, substituting the control of property with the control of "decision-making authority," then include *holistic value* in that process just as we did for property valuation and exchange. And thus we arrive at the most intimate kernel of the individual freedom vs. collective responsibility dynamic. In more advanced and sophisticated orientations, moral creativity equates the two. That is the political expression of the *unitive principle*: as our morality evolves, any intention, decision, action or social structure that facilitates individual freedom is increasingly enabled through collective responsibility, and any intention, decision, action or social structure that establishes collective responsibility is grounded in a profound appreciation individual freedom and its routine reification. Thus, in the unitive frame, individual freedom is always a collective responsibility.

This equation is evident in the transition from childhood to adulthood in virtually all cultures. Why do we sacrifice some small portion of personal freedom when we enter a committed romantic relationship? Out of love for our partner. Why do we sacrifice a bit more latitude in available choices when we have children? Out of love for our children. Why do we agree to sacrifice a weekend to help a friend who is ill, or relocating, or getting married? Because we love our friends. And why do we, if we are indeed morally mature, sacrifice a handful of additional options in our personal actions when we conform to society's rule of law? Because we love our fellow citizens. An immature person might do all of these things out of fear of abandonment or rejection, or out of a mistrustful attempt to gain advantage, or out of a guilt-ridden sense of obligation, or because they are afraid of being punished for disobeying the law. But a mature person is grounded in affectionate compassion for an ever-enlarging sphere of interconnected awareness, and thus their heart grows to include more and more beyond the tiny, egoic self. It is the tiny, egoic self, after all, that conceives of freedom as being able to do anything we want, without regard to the impact of our actions on the world around us.

This leads us to a more comprehensive view of why Aristotle is convinced that a virtuous person *acts for their friend's sake, and sacrifices their own interest...even if no one knows about it.* As previously alluded to, the breadth of moral creativity guided by such an assumption extends far beyond a few legalistic dos and don'ts, and into a high plane of insightful wisdom about how best to love and serve our fellow human beings. The aim of a morally mature society is to establish a world in which loving, nourishing, enriching actions are supported and augmented through collective agreement, by all and for all. It is a society in which "just, humble, kind, generous, judicious, self-controlled acts that benefit of others without expectation of reciprocation or reward" are the tacitly understood and explicitly celebrated aim. It is the fundamental, unshakeable belief that all human beings can pass through a self-absorbed childhood into an empowered, capable, caring adulthood where *agape* becomes a natural reflex. And it is the appreciation that humanity is passing through a vast ocean of transformation for a reason - even if that reason is only a process of growing up as individuals, as a cohesive society, as a proud species of planet Earth, or as a contributive consciousness to the Universe itself.

Now let's return to the relationship of self to decision-making authority, using our Levels as a guide. My take would be that failed states (primitive anarchistic) reside at Level 2, despotic regimes land somewhere around Level 2 or Level 3, highly centralized authoritarian regimes around Level 3 or Level 4, immature democracies around Level 5, presidential democracies around Level 6, mature parliamentary democracies around Level 7, direct democracies that are still dependent on large civic institutions around Level 8, and direct democracies with less dependence on large civic institutions (evolved anarchistic) around Level 9. These are only approximations that probably stretch the *property position* metaphor to its limit, but they hold up surprisingly well. And since a broad swath of the approaches described thus far specifically address ecological impact concerns, it also seems useful to include the moral orientation of each approach to the environment as well. For simplicity, this is mainly captured in how a particular approach relates to *wild things*. Here, then, is a high-altitude snapshot, keeping in mind how these approaches have expressed themselves in their extant, real world ranges where we can:

Table: Moral Function in Political Economies

		Mean Expectation of Moral Function		
		Economic System	Philosophy of Government	Environmental Orientation
Ideological Approach	Marxist-Leninist; single-party, centralized authority socialism	Level 6	Level 3 to Level 4	Level 3 to Level 4
	U.S.-style, market-centric mixed-economy; pluralistic, representative, constitutional, presidential democracy	Level 4	Level 6	Level 6 to Level 7
	Canadian & European mixed-economy; constitutional, parliamentary democracies	Level 6	Level 7	Level 6 to Level 7
	Despotic capitalism	Level 3	Level 2	Level 3
	Market socialism (e.g. worker-cooperatives)	Level 6 to Level 7	Level 6 to Level 7	Variable
	Gift/Grant economies	Level 7 to Level 8	Unknown	Unknown
	Market-centric Libertarianism	Level 3 to Level 4	Level 8 ideal vs. Level 2 reality?	Level 4 to Level 5
	Libertarian socialism	Level 7	Level 8 (perhaps Level 9?)	Level 7
	Eco-centric experiments (EcoVillages, etc.)	Level 6 to Level 7	Level 6 to Level 7	Level 7 to Level 8

What is striking upon reviewing this table is that many established political economies present imbalances between their dominant economic system, philosophy of government, and environmental orientations. We can also observe that a "mean expectation of moral function" does not always correlate with realities on the ground. All of this inevitably creates conflicts and contradictions among systems and institutions, which historically have tended to perpetuate and polarize tensions rather than resolve into higher order moral orientations. This echoes imbalanced nourishment of any scope, where some dimensions advance while others languish; our goal, then, should be to bring them into balance. What will always be the case along these lines is that the lowest common denominator of moral function in a major social structure will hamper other, higher order expressions within a given culture. That is certainly what we have seen happen in the United States. Whenever there is a collective vision to transcend lower moral valuations, America's market-centric constituents apply ruthless pressure to undermine that vision. Despite this, because of morally evolving democratic will, many visions nevertheless succeed in governmental or non-profit civic institutions, and endure for a time. We saw the largest surge of this in the U.S. during the New Deal era, but it has occurred intermittently since the country's independence. Yet even with New Deal and other Level 6 systems and institutions that have endured for fifty years or more, we can observe an almost constant effort to erode those advances. And where does that erosive impulse originate? Almost exclusively from advocates of market-centric philosophies. So it seems clear that as we advance the level of moral function among a given populace to the highest stratum that can be implemented and sustained within its democracy, we must also better harmonize and align the philosophy of government, the economic system and the environmental orientation, in order to preserve that evolution.

One observation about the relationship between "environmental orientation" and the "mean expectation of moral function" is that this is really an indication of how *holistic value* is appreciated in each moral stratum. *Wild things* are, after all, just one of many externalities in a market-centric worldview, but become much more important in economies reflecting a higher level of moral function. So the leap we have made is that those higher levels include greater appreciation of *holistic value* in all areas. The *unitive principle* is thereby including more and more variables into that valuation process; as I/Me/Mine attenuates as the primary consideration, everything else increases in importance. Thus the breadth, depth and specificity of *holistic value* becomes more skilled as moral creativity is perfected.

So...if this moral progression is real, then the question now becomes how we can structure political economy to reflect more sophisticated moral orientations, and entice a population with diverse levels of development to consistently participate. It seems to me that we are faced with three choices:

1. Dismantle the current status quo and replace it with either an unproven ideal - or an experimental ideal that has had limited real-world testing - which embodies a higher expectation of moral function and disables rewards for unsophisticated moral strata. This would be built from the ground up with new systems and institutions. We might call this *radical revolution.*

2. Make major structural and systemic changes to the current status quo, with an aim to contain influences from lower moral valuation strata and support higher levels of moral function. We could achieve this by substantially reshaping existing systems and institutions with ideals that have either had limited

real-world testing, and/or are experimental pilot programs. We might call this *rapid systemic reform.*

3. Make microadjustments within the current status quo that incentivize more sophisticated moral function, and penalize or otherwise restrict function in the lowest moral strata, using existing mechanisms and institutions. We might call this *incremental adjustment.*

In discussing these choices, there are a few underlying assumptions that history instructs us to maintain. The first is that whatever change is desired, it cannot be imposed authoritatively from the top down - change agency must be democratically supported, and democratically maintained over time, in order to succeed. The rule of law remains important to restrict those outliers who still revel in lower moral strata, but the ideal relationship between government and populace would be the mutual championing of agreed-upon ideals. The second assumption is that, for any substantive shift to endure, a fair bit more than half of an electorate must continually support it; this is true in direct democracies, distributed democratic systems, and representative democracies. The third assumption is that a clear understanding of existing problems with the status quo, and a clear vision for what will replace it, *become common knowledge in the general populace.* The fourth is that different variations of any solution will of necessity be tailored for different populations by those populations, depending on economic status, resource availability, current level of collective moral function, educational sophistication, cultural traditions and so on. And finally, it must also be appreciated by everyone involved in the transformation process that there will be vigorous resistance from two predictable minorities: the current elite power brokers in society, and those whose native conservatism mistrusts all change.

Regarding the three options for change, it seems to me that our choice will depend in large part on the perceived urgency for transformation, the intensity of coordinated resistance to change, and the distance between where in the moral spectrum the current status quo operates, and where the democratic majority desires it to be. In the U.S., the frustration with the status quo has been exacerbated by growing concern that if something isn't done soon, the destructive impacts of market-centric, feudalistic capitalism on both the planet and societal cohesion will be irreversible. For folks who also believe that oligarchic resistance to such change is far too entrenched and powerful for any other approach, *radical revolution* becomes the only viable option. For other Americans, whose sense of urgency is lessened by pleasurable distractions or a more muted perception of both risks and the entrenchment of power, *incremental adjustment* seems like an acceptable choice. This perspective has been reinforced by progressive policies like the Affordable Care Act, which seem to indicate that *incremental adjustment* is actually occurring. In addition, there are already well-developed visions, such as "social democracy," that conform to an incremental ideal.

In my view, for the U.S. at least, the most responsible choice is the middle way of *rapid systemic reform*. Why? For one, the urgency is indeed great, as the tipping point for environmental disruption and collapse on a global scale is either rapidly approaching or is already underway, and the cultural destruction resulting from market-centric mechanisms continues to amplify itself on a global scale. For another, the tenor of elite resistance has occasionally become less confident, and somewhat desperate and shrill, whenever the cultural momentum away from commercialist corporationism becomes more pronounced. And, as we saw in the 2008 and 2012 presidential elections, the seeds of a more developed moral creativity are already present in a majority of the electorate. But why not *radical revolution*? Well, I would say that if *rapid systemic reform* fails, *radical revolution* is all that remains. But I view that as a final option, held in reserve, because of the potential disruption to the well-being of millions, perhaps billions of people that such a tumultuous transition would undoubtedly entail. At least, that is what history teaches us about such revolutions. There is also the question of whether any means justifies an end, or if the means is itself indicative of how the end will manifest; in other words, that a violent revolt will just lead to a violently repressive regime, or that top-down imposition of liberation from state-centric controls just leads to a new menu of new state-centric controls. We must take pains, it seems to me, to differentiate fierceness of our love from the fierceness of our ego, as the latter is sure to pollute the former. Although I can understand the ends-justifies-means reasoning championed by Alinsky and others, I believe there is a more effective balance to be struck. For example, I was impressed to witness the methods and general tone of the Occupy Movement, and sill have faith that such an effort could, under the right conditions and with clearer objectives, induce meaningful change. Regardless, at the present time we have a window - albeit a window that is rapidly closing - to attempt an authentic middle way.

Our further discussion of such a transition will remain focused on the U.S., because that is the environment I know best. As a preface, I enjoy the concept of "design principles" I have encountered in the Permaculture literature and the work of Elinor Ostrom, so I'll be approaching this topic in a similar way. What follows is an overview of the design principles I believe are necessary for transitioning the U.S. to a Level 7 political economy, with some proposed change targets for how those principles could be implemented. Why Level 7? For one, because the most morally advanced political economies, mainly those in Northern Europe, are already hovering at the edges of Level 7, with only a bit of fine tuning to achieve greater internal harmony. For another, I think Level 7 is probably the best we can hope for in the short run, mostly because values hierarchies in the U.S. are so far out of balance at the present time.   In the long run, I would expect to see progress to Level 8 or 9, if only to facilitate, in the far distant future, a Level 10 political economy - or its unitive equivalent in that structureless aeon.

Before I offer more details, I want to address the pervasive bias of my approach, and that is the necessity of a democratic mixed economy (i.e. possessing both market and central planning elements), as an ultimately temporary but nevertheless long-term solution.   Why?   In part, because all of the most stable, enduring, successful and morally sophisticated political economies in the real world have been democratic mixed economies.   However, I believe the "mix" should strongly favor centrally coordinated but broadly distributed worker-owned cooperatives, along with more carefully regulated markets than can generally be found today.   In addition, I believe all of this should be governed with a much stronger element of direct democracy.   I owe much of my thinking along these lines to Alex Nove's *The Economics of Feasible Socialism Revisited.* To those who would point to the limitations and failures of state-centric designs, I would emphasize that I am not advocating that approach at all.   I am trying to chart much different territory here.   As examples of the first stages of transition, I would once again point to Germany and Switzerland, where mixed economies marry elements of democratic socialism and free markets.   Yet neither of these implementations go quite far enough.

To understand the success of mixed economies, we need to appreciate why components of both central planning and public exchange markets are so important for any interim solution.   Although I am sympathetic with anarchistic ideas of self-organized, self-determining networks of collectives, I believe this vision relies too heavily on a number of conditions that have yet to occur.   One of those conditions is a broad base of homogenous moral function, with widely shared values hierarchies. Without omnipresent agreement across all of society, there is no way to ensure that, for example, standards of ownership and distribution of both property and decision-making authority will be maintained. Another critical condition is that without an equally pervasive and equitable system of distributed production, there will always be concentration of production and its necessary economies of scale. Not for everything, mind you, but for many key industries that have already become universal; not for autonomous creation of higher layer intangible property, or the development of social capital, but for the age-old tangible staples that support all of civilization, and which mainly inhabit the lower OSI *abstraction* layers.

For those staples, although we can envision the localized sourcing and sharing of food and alternative energy, via community cooperatives and the like, there is still the issue of asymmetric and idiosyncratic production and consumption. Water, agriculture and energy production are inevitably concentrated in the geographic areas most suitable or resource-rich, then made available to every community, or even every household, over an ever more ubiquitous inhabited geography. And that habitation has become urbanized and highly concentrated as well, further exaggerating the disconnect between production and consumption. In addition, certain communities will produce or consume more than others, as influenced by culture, expected standards of living, work ethic, and so forth. These are all well-established trends, driven by exponential population growth, new and existing sub-cultures, and the increasingly refined and diverse appetites of a technological society. Without a sudden and unlikely reversal in these trends, the necessary efficiencies of large-scale production and distribution are impossible to replace with more distributed, localized alternatives; we can certainly shift some production in this direction, but not all.

The same could be said of certain services. For example, voice and data networks have indeed created the illusion of distributed technological autonomy. But, in reality, hugely concentrated public and private investments were required to create a technology backbone to support those services, and that backbone continues to rely on centralized coordination and administration.

At the same time, large, heterogeneous competitive markets create unique incentives that really can't be replicated by either centrally planned systems or insular, intentional community economies. Whether through innovation or improved quality, production efficiency or rewarding risks, competitive markets consistently energize human creativity and problem solving in powerful ways. At the same time, competition has delivered many antagonistic impacts as well, as we will discuss in the last section of the book. Which is why that competition must be organized and managed in such a way that the least desirable results can be attenuated. For example, consider the health insurance industry in Switzerland. Insurance providers are non-profit organizations whose administrative overhead is fixed by the state. However, they compete in the insurance marketplace for the same pool of consumers, engineering the best possible insurance products and services they can to win their share of customers. Here we see little of the bureaucratic rigidity of government-run health plans - and even less of the excessive profits or perverse incentives of less regulated competitive healthcare. The heart of our problem isn't competition or central planning, it is "the rules of the game" governing how that competition and planning express themselves in a given context. It seems to me that understanding the most beneficial game rules should be the primary concern of any design - rather than insisting on ideological purity - and so we will want to integrate the best ideas each perspective has to offer.

When three-dimensional - or even four-dimensional - printers are a common household appliance, and large scale industries can be scaled with small worker-cooperatives; when the global population has stabilized, and all of Earth's natural resources can be cultivated and distributed in a sustainable and equitable fashion; when humanity has embraced distributed renewable energy, and privatized monopolies have been all but eliminated; when communication and perhaps even transportation devices operate with quantum connectivity, and water can be produced anywhere cheaply; when these advances and their cascading consequences have become the status quo, then more spontaneous, rhizomatic models will inevitably prevail. We have already seen the rise of peer to peer synergies, networked intelligence, and non-hierarchical social movements as a prominent feature in cultures around the globe. Anarchistic political economies, once relegated to fringe intellectuals, have also gained a modicum of mainstream appreciation and legitimization. None of this is new, but the level of acceptance and application - and indeed the global utilization for effective change agency - is stunning in its scale.

Along the same lines, I also foresee a time when a one-way gift or grant economy is the dominant economy on the planet, and when a "post-scarcity" orientation is not reliant on abundant resources, per se, but is simply an abundant state of mind. Right now we can only model this as best we can. What we must first perfect is a long-term transition that allows for all these eventualities to slowly but inexorably take shape. And so my hope is that many, if not all, of these prerequisite conditions can be achieved through a carefully balanced, mixed economy that retains centralized standards, systems and supportive structures, but implements those standards, systems and structures through highly distributed self-governance. Thus, although complexity is still organized on a large scale, it is tactically managed on a small scale.

Design Principles of a Level 7 Political Economy

At the highest levels of organization, the objectives of a Level 7 political economy look something like this:

- A philosophy of government that more fluidly and directly expresses democratic will, and does so equally, inclusive of all ideological orientations and special interests, without disproportionate influence through concentrations of material wealth or social capital.

- An economic system that inherently enables the most equitable, egalitarian distribution of material wealth and social capital, and provides the same opportunities for all potential and existing producers of goods and services. This system sustains itself in a stable, high quality steady state - or reliable cycles of ebb and flow - rather than depending on constant growth.

- An education system that supports all other systems with a diversely informed populace trained in compassion, critical thought, alternative viewpoints and broad-spectrum dialogue; that is, a populace whose literacy and interests can manage economies and governments from an advanced moral orientation.

- A mediasphere that offers a level playing field for the emergence of divergent perspectives, while at the same time providing both democratically controlled feedback mechanisms for accuracy and fairness, and ubiquitous access to independent evaluative data on all sources of information.

- An industrial production system that not only strives toward an equitable distribution of profits and decision-making within each organization, but also incorporates social, political and ecological externalities into its strategic and tactical metrics and decisions, for the greatest benefit to all.

- An energy production system that relies on highly distributed, scalable, renewable resources whose capacities in a steady-state, cyclical, non-growth economy inherently exceed demand as both conservation and efficiencies increase over time.

- A monetary system that does not, by its very nature, create inflationary pressures, perpetual debt-slavery, or concentration of wealth in private banks, but instead encourages investment opportunities for all, while remaining under public democratic control.

- All of these principles would derive from a primary objective to encourage *property positioning* that a) moves most property into *public domain* and *common ownership*; b) incorporates *holistic value* into all planning and transactions (with the goal that exchange value would strongly correlate with *holistic value* in all markets); and c) stabilizes all of the lower property layers so that spontaneous productivity of *session layer* property and above may thrive.

- In all of these contexts, initial policies and rigorous metrics would strive to maintain a continuous Pareto efficiency, as framed by the intention that public goods eventually overtake most arenas of private profit.

I don't believe these are difficult to achieve...if we ground our design, leadership, communication and implementation in a Level 7 moral orientation. Of course this is a chicken-and-egg challenge, for in order to arrive through more sophisticated moral valuations, we often need the safety and support of societal structures that already reflect them. Each element of *rapid systemic reform* is a self-perpetuating memeplex that informs our selfplex, which in turn promotes and expands the memeplex. It's difficult to escape this loop. But we must begin somewhere, so here are a few change targets I believe would accelerate the vitality of both the chicken and the egg in the U.S.A.:

1. To whatever degree possible, quid pro quo political connections between industry, finance, a more direct democratic implementation of government, the mediasphere, the education system, and the health-and-welfare system must be severed, then insulated from each other as rigorously as possible. These are of course interdependent structures, but separation could be maintained through independent funding, governance processes and decision-making cycles, with differing degrees of direct democratic involvement (or insertion of the democratic process at different junctures in the governance process, so as to counterbalance short-lived collective impulses). What we are aiming for here is a pragmatic, clearly boundarized, functional and political separation. The final purveyor of this separation is of course the

general populace, but that democratic will would be concentrated and normalized through different formulas and durations of leadership - as well as staggered referendum cycles and legal restrictions on revolving door employment across divisions.

2. Although central government would still consist of executive, legislative and judicial branches, the two-party system would of necessity be abolished. Instead, the legislative branch would be restructured to reflect either a parliamentary system, or some other effective means of proportional representation. In addition, more frequent direct national referendums would guide public policy at the national level, so that procedural sabotage of democracy (such as the current "majority of the majority" rule in the House of Representatives) could be overridden. Likewise, direct votes at each level of government, all the way down to local, would inform policy and practice at those levels. A certain percentage of government representatives could also be chosen at each level of government through a service lottery, much as jury duty selections occur today, to serve for a limited time as part of decision making bodies (citizen commissions, city councils, state legislatures, etc.). And a certain percentage of representatives would be selected through a multi-party election process without primaries, to serve for longer terms than those selected via lottery, but with a limit on the number of terms they could serve. It should be understood and appreciated that highly advanced societies will require highly specialized skill sets for these elected officials, and that many independent schools of technocratic proficiency will inevitably arise to meet this need. The key will be to ensure that all such specialized viewpoints are adequately represented.

3. Labor would be separated into two distinct categories
    that would be organized and managed in different
    ways. The first category would be "infrastructure
    and essential services." These are the fundamental
    products and services necessary for any sort of
    complex society to function at the most basic levels
    (i.e. lower OSI *abstraction* layers), and which have
    already tended to be socialized in most mixed-
    economies. Roads, bridges, water, electricity and
    communication are the first tier of this category,
    followed by more abstracted products and services
    that build on those foundations, but are still
    perceived as universal expectations by the general
    public. This second tier is comprised of the systems
    and institutions that provide the backbone of civil
    society. For example, public transportation, public
    healthcare, public education, public safety services,
    social security, and so on. As expectations differ
    from one zeitgeist to the next, so would the scope of
    inclusion in these tiers. I happen to think basic
    banking and insurance services, basic nutrition,
    basic housing, mail delivery, worker retraining,
    employment placement services, and unemployment
    benefits also fall under "infrastructure and essential
    services." One common thread of these *public
    domain* industries, however, is that they facilitate
    trade for the second category of labor. This is a
    crucial point: without centrally coordinated
    infrastructure and essential services, there really is
    no way to enable a reliable (or equitable) exchange
    economy of any kind.

To whatever degree possible, *all of this should be
organized and tactically managed at the community
level*, with centralized standardization and support,
subject to direct democratic control. Instead of
centrally run state institutions or corporations, there
would be **networked, non-profit, worker-owned**

cooperatives that are centrally regulated but monitored and executed at the community level. It might also be interesting for different regions to compete with each other for customer satisfaction levels, and be rewarded in some way for their success. If the service or product being delivered is of the *physical layer*, there wouldn't be competition for customers between the cooperatives, but the cooperatives would be limited in size (by service area, etc.), and subject to public input and scrutiny to ensure an adequate level of service delivery. If the service or product is of the *network layer* or higher, then the non-profit cooperatives could compete with each other for the same customers across different regions. So although there is a strong element of central planning here, the actual control and execution is highly segmented and distributed, both because of the divisions of government already alluded to, and the emphasis on community-level organization.

There should be some mechanism to ensure this foundation doesn't somehow undermine individual contribution to society by inoculating the least morally developed against survival or well-being concerns. That is, there must be some form of citizen reciprocation for this foundation, and consequences for a lack of reciprocation. So, for instance, everyone who receives these benefits could participate in these very same programs as unpaid volunteers for short but regular periods of time, with consistent expectations of performance. If someone chooses not to volunteer, or willfully demonstrates exceedingly poor performance, their access to some or all of these services (or perhaps certain qualities of service) could be restricted.

4. The second category of labor is for production of goods and services that add value to society above and beyond essential services. There would be several tiers to this category. At the top would be certain major industries, especially those that a) have essentially become closed to rapid or major innovation, b) are de facto market monopolies, or c) otherwise dictate economies of scale with highly centralized controls. These would become worker-owned cooperatives subject to governmental oversight, with the level of government responsible for oversight always larger than the size and reach of the business itself. These would be much like the first category of labor, but in this case for-profit. There is no reason why this tier couldn't compete with cooperatives in the first category, wherever that makes sense. Again, the scope of this category will change from one culture to the next, and from one generation to the next.

In the second tier we find medium-to-large businesses, once again worker-owned cooperatives, which would compete with each other for customers. Communities in which either of these two top-tier businesses are located would have the ability to a) reject proposals to start a business in a given location, b) introduce progressive penalties on a misbehaving or undesirable business in their community, or c) rescind a business's privilege to operate in their community altogether. All of this would be accomplished through a direct referendum process, with the intent that all such businesses work closely with the community to address that community's preferences and concerns. The third tier would be sole proprietorships or very small businesses (perhaps five employees or less?), which is the only tier where a business entity could be privately owned. This three-tier system - or an equivalent approach - is an absolute necessity, in my view, since currently such huge concentrations of wealth and influence in private corporations has demonstrated itself to be the greatest threat to a functional democracy, the most pernicious abuser and exploiter of workers and the environment, and the most disruptive to our collective moral maturation process. In other words, these huge privatized industries are simply too powerful to be permitted to exist outside of the democratic process as they do today.

5. The ratio between the salary of the highest paid individuals in a given field and that of the lowest paid individuals in the same field - as well as what the highest and lowest wages would be, the benefits of seniority, and other aspects of pay structure - could be publicly set through a direct democratic process by the general populace for all businesses that are not privately owned (i.e. for all businesses except sole proprietorships and very small businesses). The same formula could be applied to the ownership of communal property shares. To avoid rapid salary swings, changes could be incremented over time. In addition, the highest and lowest wages across all of society could also be democratically set to reflect their *holistic value* as evaluated and agreed upon by the electorate. In both cases, this wage-setting process could be repeated regularly every few years. Using some combination of consistent calculation factors, this would reflect a more equitable distribution of wages within organizations and across whole industries, especially as some positions between those organizations become interchangeable. To include a competitive variable in this equation, profit-sharing would not be part of these set wages, but in addition to it. However, profit-sharing could also be distributed

according to exactly the same wage ratio. There could of course be other profit distribution mechanisms, but the goal is to curtail the stratospheric concentration of wealth in any individual or group of individuals.

6. As an important *holistic value* consideration, trades that fall within the *perverse utility* categorization would be subject to train-test-monitor controls. This is more fully discussed in the next section, but is important because these particular trades tend to erode social cohesion and moral evolution. Along the same lines, human interaction with the Earth's ecosystems must be compassionate, sustainable and low-or-no impact. I appreciate the core tenets and twelve design principles of the Permaculture movement, and think they provide an excellent starting point here. Further, the "precautionary principle" would guide all technology development and deployment.

7. Energy from renewable resources could be produced locally whenever possible, via community cooperatives, and ideally using business and residential structures as installation platforms, then aggregated and distributed within each geographic region as needed. The absolute end of fossil fuel and other nonrenewable energy production must be aggressively, rapidly and relentlessly pursued. This is not only for the sake of eliminating carbon emissions, but also because the very nature of concentrated-yield sources like petroleum distorts consumption expectations and reduces costs in the short term, while the long term reality of stable, steady-state energy sourcing dictates entirely different consumption and cost relationships. Local-renewable approaches align with the longer term energy expectations, and mirror the distributed

nature of production, labor and political power in this new political economy.

8. Part of a fundamental education should, I would think, be the inclusion of many of the concepts addressed in this book, with an emphasis on comprehensive training in full-spectrum nourishment, synergistic dialogue, moral creativity and development, and an overview of the strengths and failings of various political economies. And of course students, parents and teachers should all share responsibility for the structure and management of a more participatory educational environment. I also believe exposure to other cultures has extraordinary benefit for the young, and to that end every child should have the opportunity to experience for themselves how the rest of the world lives, ideally by traveling to and living among other cultures. In fact, this is probably a critical foundation for appreciating diverse viewpoints, navigating social complexities, and learning to think multidimensionally. It seems the broader and deeper the vocabulary of language, ideas and experiences made available to our young people, the more likely they will be able to manage complex responsibilities for the rest of their lives. But the intent behind all of these approaches should be to encourage the advanced moral function necessary to sustain the political economy proposed here.

9. The importance of civic institutions and social movements that arise spontaneously - often operating independently of both markets and government - should also be recognized and vigorously facilitated. These not only fill gaps in needed services and resources, but may provide unexpected change agency toward a higher moral function in society. In particular, community

development corporations (CDCs) and community land trusts (CLTs), when guided by community input and participation, offer a promising mode of communal transformation. At the same time, institutions that become well-established players in civil society should also be subject to direct democratic control - just as government, non-profit and commercial enterprises would be under this proposal.

10. Clearly some attention must also be given to reforming the tax code. In market-centric economies like the U.S., taxes are often used to incentivize some behaviors while penalizing others. This tool should no longer be needed to the same degree, and the tax code could be substantially simplified as property ownership - and the surplus value of production - advances into more unitive strata. As an interim step, a progressively tiered tax rate with very few deductions should work for individuals, along with a similarly tiered tax rate on net income for businesses, based on their size. In conjunction with this, a flat rate "wealth tax" could be implemented across the board to augment and perhaps even replace income taxes. As property position shifts, this wealth tax, in turn, could increasingly be calculated on accumulated shares of communal property.

11. The monetary system should be subject to the direct control of the people as a socialized central bank, in conjunction with a national network of non-profit cooperatives and community banking systems. For-profit lending institutions could be entirely eliminated, and fractional reserve banking would, at a minimum, be strictly restrained by a conservative leverage ratio - one that is either set in stone or can only be adjusted to be more conservative, not less.

Government institutions would no longer pay interest on any loan, and indeed a set percentage of government loans would be lent interest-free to large scale entrepreneurs, non-profit community organizations, community land trusts and worker-cooperatives, in order to stimulate innovation, create a level playing field for emerging disciplines and technologies, and instigate a road to self-sufficiency. Special targeting of "outsider" innovation would be an ideal standard, but realistically this may have to be left to the market side of the mix. There is also opportunity here to institute a gift economy with a certain percentage of government lending as well, and this should increase over time as society matures (that is, as society demonstrates the *unitive principle* in perpetual and reciprocal gift giving across multiple OSI layers).

12. One of the consequences of monetary reform would be the elimination of the stock market as it exists today. It is difficult to conceive of any sort of stock exchange scenario that can't be exploited, or that doesn't contribute to market instability, as has been evidenced many times over in the U.S., and has only increased with the advent of automated computer trades. That said, there should probably be some opportunity for stock trades to occur, so that outsider innovations and other market advantages can be facilitated in emerging industries. However, the resulting stock exchange system would be of a much smaller scale than its current manifestation, and would be looked upon more as an interesting experiment than a central feature of the economy. There could also be strict restrictions on highly speculative investment instruments, and perhaps a small tax on every trade, to further contain volatility and reduce impact on the rest of the economy.

13. It may also be useful to either institute or promote different kinds of currency that operate mainly within different dimensions of the economy; for example, there could be gift dollars, market exchange dollars, public utility dollars, barter systems, community banking systems, and other currency independent of fiat money. These could still be sanctioned and coordinated through the central bank, or just be encouraged and supported through independent institutions, so that morally advanced experiments demonstrate proof-of-concept.

14. In order for any of these ideas to retain integrity and resist corruption in a fully functional democracy, the electorate must have access to both raw data and complex analysis tools about virtually every element of society. Whether it be a judge's rulings history, a manufacturer's product safety record, or a politician's legislative patterns, multidimensional data on every individual and institution in public life should be readily available via the web at no cost. In addition, users should be able to specify values criteria that represent their priorities, and dynamically display data according to those personal criteria. A standardized analysis tool could be provided across several competing information sources: nonprofit government-run clearinghouses, community-based information providers, and mass media news outlets.

What is the litmus test for the success of these or any other design principles? In my view it should be whether the twelve dimensions are being fully nourished both individually and collectively. In other words, does every person have the opportunity and resources available for full-spectrum nourishment? Are there time, space and resources within organizations for people to nourish all dimensions? Are these dimensions expressed in the way

systems and institutions operate? Is space, time, energy
and intention continually being created in society to
nourish, grow and transform all dimensions? Is there
evidence of an all-encompassing love-consciousness
permeating the relationships between individuals and
institutions, and between institutions and the natural
environment? If so, does all of this result in the kind of
property positioning already outlined as a primary objective?

Diagram: Level 7 Proposals

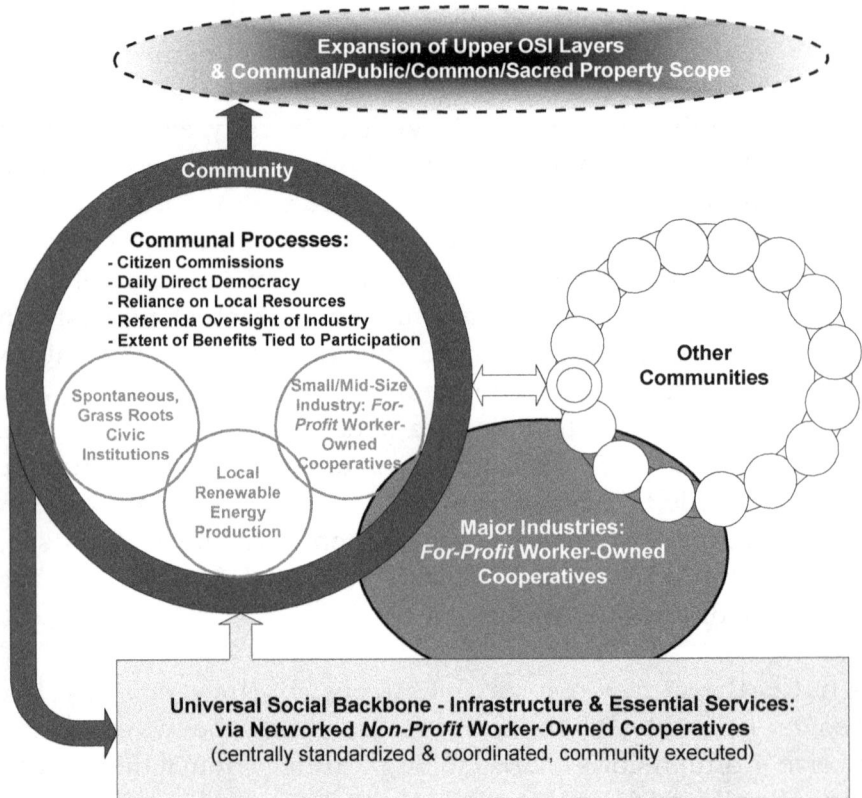

In the U.S. and many other developed countries, an
amendable federal Constitution embodies the dynamic

moral creativity of its population, as well as its changing level of moral development, and many of the changes I've proposed would require revisions to the U.S. Constitution. However, in many if not all cases, other civic institutions will define, inculcate and perpetuate their particular brand of moral creativity. And sometimes these institutions may be at odds with the values hierarchies represented in the Constitution, or the current manifestations of markets and government. For example, in the U.S., many religious institutions view themselves as purveyors of moral creativity, but find themselves at odds with each other, with federal and state Constitutions, or with how the law of the land is enforced. In a similar vein, since at least the industrial revolution large corporations have systematically subverted many U.S. Constitutional values in favor of egocentric brutality, cronyism and the exploitation of people and resources. Then we have organizations like the National Resource Defense Council or the American Civil Liberties Union, which believe they are championing certain constitutional values in their own unique way. So we cannot discount the importance of these structures in civil society, or the role they play in its evolution.

In some ways, the incomplete expression (or outright corruption) of moral creativity by some civic institutions illustrates anarchist concerns that authoritative structures persistently aim to empower themselves, while depriving citizens of individual freedoms. At the same time, if all of these civic elements are subject to democratic controls - and the electorate is allowed to be educated and informed, and able to hold itself aloof from special interest propaganda - the result is a dynamic synthesis of different perspectives and priorities. And, as unfortunate as it may be, a fairly large central government is one of the only practical ways to implement "infrastructure and essential services" that support a truly democratic civil society, a functional exchange economy and such diverse civic institutions. The key seems to be accountability and flexibility of that central government, and the diffusion (distribution) of its power. All of this can be achieved through elements of direct democracy, the insulated divisions of government, and the emphasis on community-level decision making already described. Although this can and should be embodied in a revised Constitution, it ultimately must also be echoed in all of the institutions and economies that comprise civil society, so that the moral function of every element of that society can harmonize with every other. Again, however, this will ultimately depend upon a more pervasive sophistication of moral creativity in the populace itself.

I do believe that, someday, the natural evolution of society via the *unitive principle* will lead to more rhizomatic expressions of political economy from top to bottom (i.e. in all levels of civil society, and all layers of property *abstraction*). Until that time, however, it is unrealistic to assume that many of the lower OSI layers can be accomplished without economies of scale, and the modicum of natural monopolization and central planning that inherently occurs along with this. Both production and decision-making authority can still be distributed to the community level, and/or managed through a direct democratic process, but there remains a strong element of hierarchical control among these lower OSI layers. For *session layer* and above, I think opportunities abound to break free of such hierarchy - in fact it's already happening. But, as mentioned previously, we can't forget the foundation required to enable this dynamically creative environment. Once again, individual freedom is a collective responsibility; in this case, the collective agreement to maintain foundational structures (i.e. lower OSI layers) so that higher order, spontaneous and indeed revolutionary expressions of both property and decision-making authority can thrive unhindered.

The Organic Diffusion of Wealth and Power

We really zero in on the heart of a sustainable political economy when we explore ideal ways to distribute wealth and power, and the core of that distributive vision is organization and empowerment at the community level. Why emphasize efforts at that level? Because communities where people know and care about each other provide an ideal scale for democratic decision-making; a direct democracy that can be compassionate, viable and accountable. The core of community-based proposals is a simple principle: communal engagement with every variable that impacts members of that community. This involvement cannot reside solely in elected representation or periodic referenda, but must also occur more directly and frequently within the electorate itself. That is, through ongoing communal decision-making, funding, and feedback mechanisms.

Consensus-based community organizing has proven a crucial component of many historic evolutions, and deserves careful consideration. But what energizes such efforts? What causes the grass to grow? Is it a sense of justice, of righting a wrong, of fairness and equality? Or is there a deeper well to draw from? When moral creativity permeates consciousness, a more complex array of motivations percolates to the fore. There is a desire to integrate perspectives, to honor outliers along within the mean, to recognize genius and create a consensus from additive synthesis, transcending the lowest common denominator without reviling it. Why? Because passionate compassion is generative, not conciliatory; it rises above the mundane even as it carries the mundane with it, so that, to borrow a phrase from Alfred Whitehead, "novelty does not mean loss." What are the building blocks for this force for good? Once again, it is my contention that love-consciousnesses is not achievable or sustainable without careful attention to full-spectrum nourishment; beginning with each individual, the twelve dimensions of well-being must be affectionately embraced and nurtured before this energy transmutes into sustainable activism.

As for institutional reforms, why not implement direct democracy at the community level? Using existing technologies, direct democracy could be regularly realized on a vast scale. Imagine a societal expectation that, every day, citizens would vote on any number of decisions with real-world consequences in their community, and do so from the comfort and convenience of their homes; we might call this "daily direct democracy." This could shape the prioritization of infrastructure funding, or zoning for certain business activities, or the number of regular police patrols in local neighborhoods, and so on. Whatever strategic or tactical concerns could easily incorporate direct democratic decision-making would be reviewed each day, and revised and adjusted as citizens observed the impact of their decisions over time. Regarding decisions where specialized knowledge is needed, votes could be organized, solicited and even weighted based on a combination of self-reported interests, expertise and experience. Imagine further that such expectations are tied to certain social privileges - that participation in governance and planning affords benefits that would otherwise be limited or unavailable.

For community issues that require more advanced, rare or specialized knowledge - and perhaps coordination across multiple tiers of government or longer decision-making cycles - community members selected through automated lotteries could participate regularly as part of citizen commissions and community development teams, each with a clearly defined scope of responsibility, interagency liaising, preparatory training, and expectation of wider public input and reporting. Such teams and commissions could work in conjunction with elected officials and established government agencies for a limited period of time, then relinquish their position to the next group of lottery appointees. As alluded to earlier, some percentage of government agency positions would be selected via lottery as well. All of this is intended to mitigate the dangers of entrenched government bureaucracies, special interest influence, and career politicians who serve their own interests above those of their constituents. Here, however, citizen participation is mandatory and regular, demanding a high baseline level of education and ongoing awareness about community concerns and governance.

All of these ideas highlight an important consideration: in order to participate effectively in their own governance, community members will require extensive knowledge in the principles of community resource management, economic development and consensus building, as well as a more rigorous continuation of that education moving forward. To this end, the lessons of past successes should inform the proposed dynamics between government agencies, citizen commissions, grass-roots organizations and direct democracy. These would include empowered community organizing, awareness and development efforts, worker/consumer-owned cooperatives that have worked well, and effective partnerships between CDCs, CLTs and the communities in which they reside. Replicating the checks and balances of the overall political economy, communities would need to integrate the technocratic proficiencies of elected positions, the efficiencies of central planning and coordination, a will of the people that is both informed and compassionate, and many of the risks and benefits of free markets.

Under the same umbrella, the labor and resources that actualize community decision-making would, to whatever degree possible, be sourced from the community itself. How can self-sufficiency in decision-making be fostered if the cost of those decisions isn't borne by the community? As already mentioned, I like the idea of incentivized public funding and participation, where those who contribute the most in terms time, resources or ideas are rewarded with a certain level of benefit from outcomes, such as a certain quality of service, or guaranteed utilization. The valuation of contributions should of course be multidimensional, so than everyone who desires to do so can contribute in some way. But those who refuse to contribute - who consistently demonstrate that they do not value civic participation - should be afforded either fewer benefits, or benefits of lower quality. In addition, wealth generation and management can itself be reframed to the community level, and CDC, CLT and other organizational models could be expanded to include all layers of OSI property abstraction.

In many ways, the specific details of community-centric visions and processes matter less than the importance of engagement and dialogue both within a community, between communities, and between each community and the regional, national and global apparatuses of economy and government. The encouragement that such interactions become more intimate rather than less is paramount. One of the most destructive disconnects of the modern age is the perpetuation of the isolated individual or family that has no relationship with their community, its government and its resources, other than through paying a fee for a service, a tax for infrastructure that is taken for granted, or a vote to empower a stranger they have never met who will make decisions for them. This distancing of cause-and-effect into non-relating, discompassionate, reflexive and often apathetic exchanges is a principle destroyer of social cohesion. To reverse this trend, we need to reconnect with each other. Still, the question persists: how do we achieve a new, more cohesive model in the most organic ways? That is, a way that isn't imposed from the top down, or purely theoretical? It's all well-and-good to champion a new vision...but how do we reify it?

This vision will require memetic propagation through multiple vectors, some of which are organic and grass roots, and others that are more hierarchical and top-down, mirroring the mixed economy model itself. On the more organic side, we have individual self-nourishment, small study groups, neighborhood organizing, and cross-cultural artistic expressions of the *unitive principle* - all educating open-minded folks, encouraging cohesion, and energizing grass roots activism. This is not about indoctrinating abstract ideals, but providing structures and processes for an extant, innate impulse; we all yearn to love, grow and thrive, to live compassionately and joyfully, but we sometimes need reminders of how to do that together, and how to call on the skills and wisdom we already have within us. If these reminders are provided through integral, community-oriented communication that appeals to every walk of life and every stage of moral development, the rising tide of consciousness truly will lift all boats.

In the next level of propagation, we have organizations of various sizes that pilot a more egalitarian, democratic and distributed forms of governance and benefits-sharing. For example, non-profit community banking systems; K-12 schools that are administered jointly by students, parents and teachers; community cooperatives that generate renewable energy; and businesses that shift from a traditional organization and ownership to worker-owned cooperatives. Then we have community level organizers, leaders and activists that initiate ad-hoc citizens commissions to champion communal decision-making. These pioneers can lobby to amend charters of established municipal and regional decision-making bodies so they incorporate communal processes. They can also create non-profit organizations that serve community interests with community input, and advocate community-centric models through other forms of change agency.

At the more centralized end of the spectrum, we have existing and proposed democratic structures that can initiate necessary reforms to government institutions. Reforms like eradicating cronyism through campaign finance restructuring, lobbying restrictions, term limits legislation and so forth. Ideally, all elections could be publicly funded, and corporate influence eradicated, via constitutional amendment. A funding program could also be developed to assist workers with worker buyouts. All of this could coincide with reforms to K-12 curricula that advance the *unitive principle*, critical thinking and mutually empowering dialogue, and enhance the esteem of multidimensional reasoning and nourishment. And of course part of that reform could include pilot programs that demonstrate the infusion of direct democracy into central planning across all divisions of government; for example, allowing USPS workers and customers, rather than Congress, to vote on Postal Service policies, priorities and employee retirement funding.

However, we know from history that such positive modeling and inculcation by itself is insufficient. Decades of successful alternative governance and economies demonstrated by planned communities, community organizing, direct democracies and worker cooperatives around the globe have not persuaded the dominant memeplex of oligarchic capitalism to make room for those alternatives. Likewise, populist movements have only nudged the established order by tiny increments. And despite the escalation of environmental degradation and illnesses linked to pollution, despite the erosion of personal freedoms and endless disgorgement of deceptive groupthink, despite the exploitation and suppression of the poorest and most desperate populations of the world and a spiraling host of other maladies, the masses either remain unmoved, or only intermittently and briefly interested. So there must also be active resistance to, and disruption of, the status quo.

There are many ways to do this. One is to attenuate the "bread and the circuses" (*panem et circenses*) that appease the masses and medicate away any desire for revolution or reform. When the society of the spectacle (Guy Debord) is first exposed and then undone - when non-relating, commoditized social life is firmly disrupted - a facilitative vacuum allows people to create more authentic connections with each other. If an emerging majority of artistic expression, mass media, sporting competitions and popular culture embodies moral creativity, inviting constructive participation in civil society as a compassionate imperative, this would go a long way toward interrupting the pleasurable distractions and manufactured crises that currently mesmerize the American electorate. It would unmask the distastefulness of complacency. Eliminating this medication will not, in and of itself, inspire the most indifferent of our citizenry to embrace civic duty, but it will allow necessary space for a long-suppressed recognition that everyone can contribute to civil society, and even enjoy doing so. Then, in conjunction with the proposed encouragement of multidimensional nourishment and moral development, fertile ground is generated for even greater liberation.

There are other avenues of activism, of course, such as making the cost of perpetuating plutocracy so painful to the plutocrats - and the alternatives so compelling - that they voluntarily relinquish control and even contribute to a solution.   In concert with such efforts are constitutional changes that deprive corporations of a fictional "personhood" status in law, restructure legislatures into a more proportionately representative bodies, revoke all avenues of cronyism and neoliberal subversions of government, and enable many of the other top-down reforms already alluded to. But again, for these to happen, I suspect the creature comforts, class privileges and insulation from existential concerns enjoyed by the modern elite will require systematic interruption. For in the same way that the society of the spectacle distracts the masses from the deplorable reality of their condition, the cocoon of wealth and presumed entitlement insulates plutocrats from the horrific tragedies their opulence wreaks on the rest of the world.

Of course, most of this is speculative, a vision of what could be derived from observations of history, successful systems found in other parts of the world, what I have observed firsthand in successful organizations, all seasoned with equal parts intuition and optimism. Really, though, what do I know?   Only that, without prerequisite moral development, activism of any kind will only create new iterations of old systems and patterns with a fresh coat of paint. To escape ourselves, we must evolve ourselves. Only once we have begun that process can we shift our focus to utilizing the most effective mechanisms of change. Once we refine civility in our heart of hearts, we can begin to refine civil society.

With this in mind, here is one additional tool to shape that efficacy.   In her article, *A Ladder of Citizen Participation* (Journal of the American Planning Association, Vol. 35, No. 4, July 1969, pp. 216-224), Sherry Arnstein proposed an insightful way of describing different levels of civic engagement. The "rungs" of her ladder are self-explanatory, but suffice it to say that our goal should be to actualize our way to the top rungs of *citizen power* through civic engagement and activism, whatever form those efforts take. Anything less is, well, really just a variation on the spectacle.

Diagram: Arnstein's Ladder of Citizen Participation

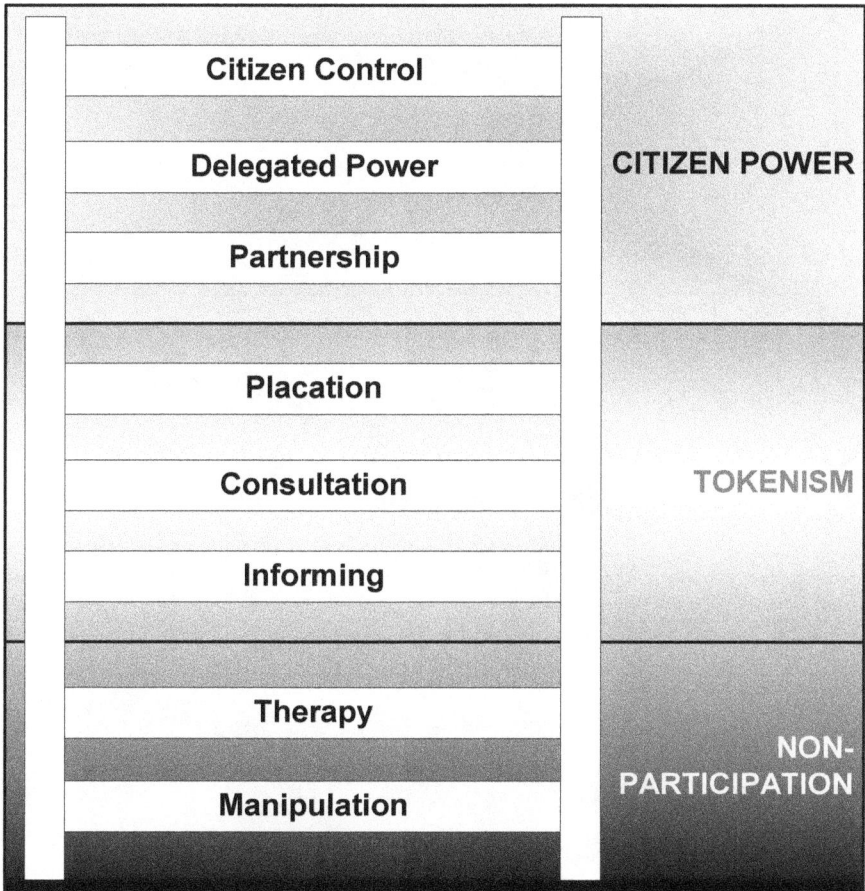

Citizen Control	
Delegated Power	**CITIZEN POWER**
Partnership	
Placation	
Consultation	**TOKENISM**
Informing	
Therapy	**NON-PARTICIPATION**
Manipulation	

As erosions to the status quo coincide with the expression of new, more compassionate structures, the *unitive principle* has opportunity to take root.   Then, as individuals, communities and whole cultures increasingly adopt responsibility for shared well-being, patterns of consumption, and the sustainable productivity of civil society, then the power and wealth of vestigial oligarchic structures will be diluted until community-centric processes overtake them entirely.

Perverse Utility and Full-Spectrum Nourishment

There remains a significant problem with any mixed economy that has not been addressed, and that is the value of goods and services that are only desirable because they either appeal to the lowest levels of moral function, or because they medicate or distract a consumer from skillful self-nourishment. That is, products with low *holistic value*, or even a negative one. In Integral Lifework, this is called "substitution nourishment," where some dimension of being is being neglected to such a degree that overcompensation occurs in other dimensions, often to an addictive extreme. It has been my hypothesis for some time that many obsessive or addictive disorders are the result of such lopsided nourishment depletion. So, from that perspective, it is especially important to address the availability and value of certain goods and services that most frequently contribute to substitution nourishment. At the same time, however, it is also of great importance to provide education and values motivation for full-spectrum nourishment, so that these substitutions are less likely to occur in the first place.

One longstanding approach to this issue has been to make certain activities or products illegal. Such is the case for certain kinds of drugs, certain types of pornography, prostitution, some forms of gambling, certain weapons and so on. The problem here, of course, is that such prohibitions tend to create an alternate economy for illicit products and services, and history has repeatedly demonstrated that a war on "X" just strengthens and expands that alternate economy, sometimes making "X" even more profitable. So a higher perceived use value results in a higher exchange value, while maintaining a low or negative *holistic value*. An alternate approach has been to legalize many of formerly illegal trades, and then tax them heavily. This has some positive benefit, in that the products and services can now be regulated and the entire trade made safer and healthier for both employees and consumers, and this also helps eliminate criminal activities and organizations (as long legalization occurs everywhere at once). In addition, such taxes are often used to fund socially productive programs like health research, treatment programs and so on. However, there is no predictable formula for which trades should be liberated from an illegal status; it seems more derived from arbitrary societal prejudices than, say, the potential harm of a product or service. For example, tobacco, caffeine and alcohol have all been legally and openly available for some time, while Psilocybin mushrooms, marijuana and amphetamines have not. Social acceptability - to the extent of widespread resistance to legal prohibitions - is really the only reason why some of these drugs are classified as legal while others aren't. But they all share they same potential for *perverse utility* in society; that is, they can all distract from authentic nourishment, or medicate depletion, rather than contribute to holistic well being.

Interestingly, taxation has also been used to penalize the production and consumption of some high-end specialty goods that are considered to be excessive in their focus on status or luxury.   Thus, in the U.S., we have both "sin" taxes and "luxury" taxes that are much higher than ordinary taxes.   So we could call all such attempts to penalize production and consumption as a *perverse utility tax*. But none of these approaches encourage full-spectrum nourishment, and indeed don't seem to curtail either the profit from such enterprises or their negative consequences. Our handling of *perverse utility* in the U.S. is almost entirely reactive rather than proactive. And yet, if we are to rely on perceived   use   value   (or   a   temporary,   subjectively experienced use value) to govern exchanges in the marketplace, don't we have to accept that different people will value things differently, and thus allow each person to make up their own mind about what risks they are willing to take? Shouldn't we just allow people to make their own mistakes and learn from them?

This is one ideal of freedom, but it ignores some fundamental truths. The first is that the extent of some risks are not obvious. In the case of the effects of certain drugs, or the way some diseases are transmitted, or even how fairly mild but continuous nutrition deficits can endanger well-being over time, ignorance can be deadly. Add to this that those who benefit from *perverse utility* trade have no incentive to educate their customers, and the increasing sophistication of packaging and marketing such goods as harmless or even healthy, and you have a perfect recipe for a free market that is highly corrosive to human welfare. In the U.S., we see the results everywhere around us. In sugary or fatty foods with little nutritional benefit marketed to children. In the excessive prescribing of SSRIs by doctors for an absurdly broad array of complaints. In potent concoctions of alcohol and caffeine whose fruity sweetness appeals to young adults.   In the plethora of mindless fads that compel adolescents to spend their parents' money.   In the equally ubiquitous pressure on adults to perpetually upgrade, improve and expand well beyond their greatest conceivable needs. The variations are endless, and ever more destructive.

So an escalating availability of options doesn't really equate freedom of choice, it just reinforces an habitual trajectory to buy bigger, better, faster and more. And legalization, regulation and taxation of the more risky, extreme or harmful forms of trade doesn't really slow that down any more than a "war" on such trade does. So what is the answer? Where can we find a model for moderating the ignorance, misinformation and imbalanced nourishment that often leads to these destructive impulses spiraling out of control? I think the answer has been staring us in the face for a long time, but, like rebellious children (or cantankerous curmudgeons?), we just don't like that answer.

How do we reduce the inherent risks of driving a heavy vehicle down a busy street, surrounded by other heavy vehicles, pedestrians, bicyclists, etc.? We have people train for a period of time, then take a test. We then use automated technologies to enforce driving safety, like cameras mounted at intersections, or under overpasses on the highway, that document violators. We also have folks who have violated traffic safety rules receive additional training in defensive driving techniques. At a certain age, we may re-test someone whose driving skills seem to be waning. In all of this, it could be argued that the education and testing is flawed, that the technology is imperfect, that a lot of folks aren't held accountable for their violations, and so on. But on the whole, with a relatively insignificant public budget, we have a system that instills standard expectations of behavior and monitors the reality. Drivers still have an immense amount of freedom, as long as they agree to abide by some very simple standards of collective responsibility.

Now let's introduce a new variable into this equation: alcohol. This drug is responsible for more accidents and vehicular fatalities than any other single factor. Just like those big, heavy, fast vehicles, alcohol can be incredibly dangerous if it is misused. And yet we approach alcohol completely differently than driving. Why? I have become increasingly convinced that this is only because alcohol has been a normalized component of many cultures for centuries. It some form, alcohol has had time to become integrated into the moral fabric of society, and so it has for the most part been allowed to "self-regulate." But anything newly introduced into society doesn't have the same benefit of hundreds of years of selective adjustment, and requires more deliberate, often provisional integration, where careful experimentation and observation determines the efficacy of different integrative approaches. Take for example the introduction of alcohol to Native American communities when Europeans first arrived in the Americas. Because this was a new, unanticipated and powerful influence, Native American culture did not have sufficient mechanisms in place to cope with it. As a result, the introduction of alcohol was disproportionately destructive to that culture.

What we have only begun to grasp in our modern era is that the industrial revolution and information age have accelerated the introduction of new, unanticipated variables into every culture. Even using alcohol as an example, the scarcity of fermented beverages prior to mass production and mass distribution placed alcohol in an entirely different category of much rarer and more valuable use that it has today. But now, anyone and everyone above a certain age can obtain alcohol in some form every day of the week, any day of the year, in any season and in almost any location. So even though alcoholic beverages have existed for millennia, they have not existed in such a widely available, potent and relatively cheap form as they do today. Our collective assumption, therefore, that alcohol usage can still "self-regulate" in the same way it did in the past is kind of silly. It's just not the same animal. The same could be said of many products and services that have evolved quickly and indeed radically in terms of their power, availability and overall impact. Think of highly lethal weapons, pharmaceuticals, petrochemicals, electromagnetic radiation, methamphetamine, fast food and smartphones.

For some new things, often the most obvious and ubiquitous new things, we have sensibly turned to the train, test and monitor model that we use for motor vehicles. But far too often we have allowed cultural assumptions carried forward from previous generations to determine our relationship with certain goods and services. What if we were to apply the training, test and monitor model to alcohol? What if, in order to even buy alcohol, it was necessary to first learn about the impact of alcohol on judgment, how it is metabolized, why it can be addictive for some people, how to identify signs of alcohol impairment or abuse, etc.? What if folks were then required to pass a test to demonstrate their understanding of such knowledge? Or to test their capacity to manage alcohol consumption, in the same way we test people's capacity to drive? And what if we then received an alcohol-usage license, which would be required to purchase alcohol of any kind? After that, alcohol purchasing could be monitored, so that excessive alcohol use could be flagged automatically. The consequences of such flagging could be the same as minor traffic infractions, ranging from small fines all the way up to mandatory training classes and alcohol abuse counseling. Again, all we are doing here is following the same training, testing and monitoring model that we use for motor vehicles...which in fact are less dangerous than alcohol in the context of both personal safety and collective responsibility to moderate our own actions for the safety of others.

This same model can be used for any *perverse utility trade*. As with a driver's license or alcohol purchasing, we already try to restrict access to pornography to those above a certain age.   Why?   Because it is viewed as risky, unhealthy, or emotionally and mentally dangerous for a young child to be exposed to certain aspects of adult sexuality, especially in an exploitative or commercialized context.   Is it as unhealthy as consuming alcohol at a young age?   Is it as dangerous as trying to drive a car? Probably not, but that does not mean understanding one's own sexuality isn't an important part of growing up, preparing for intimacy with a partner, or indeed navigating commercial   marketing   that   capitalizes   on   sexual enticement.   And, like a car or an easily available drink, the pervasive availability of pornography has introduced new variables into society that have never been there before, *changing our relationship to sexuality in unexpected ways.* For centuries, we've had strip clubs, peep shows and various manifestations of pornographic entertainment. But accessing those resources involved certain social risks, costs and benefits. When I was in my early teens in Europe this was still the case: to buy a pornographic magazine, or enter a coin-operated porn movie booth, or peruse the prostitutes displaying their wares in the Red Light district, was not a secret or private event, it was still highly public, and incurred the risks, costs and benefits that coincide with public disclosure of personal desires and interests. Whether that public disclosure was a positive or negative regulator isn't the point, the point is that it was part of an established social regulation mechanism that had existed for   many   generations.   But   this   is,   as   a   broad generalization, no longer the case.   Pornography, and indeed varieties of web-based sexual encounters, are now virtually devoid of social risks, costs or benefits; those primal urges can now operate in a self-referential bubble that has not been tested by millennia of civilization.

This is the disconnect that both rational experts and irrational reactionaries keep missing in considering these complexities: the current landscape of any *perverse utility trade* is no longer about universally shared urges, personal freedoms, select privileges or age-old dilemmas...this is *all new*. Everything has changed, and thus new approaches are required. So suppose we applied the train, test and monitor method to accessing pornography or prostitution trade, or to purchasing weapons and ammunition, or acquiring high-risk drugs? Why wouldn't it work in exactly the same way it does for automobiles? Again some may counter that there are major problems with the driver education and licensing system in the U.S., but there are other models, such as Germany's, that appear to be much more successful, and which could certainly be piloted in the U.S.

Now all of this is proposed against the backdrop of a thorough enculturation of holistic, full-spectrum models of nurturing. Whether Integral Lifework or some other form of multidimensional nourishment integration and harmonization, everyone should know how to care for themselves and contribute to the well-being of their family, peers and community at a very early age. What if every eight-year-old understood diverse avenues of intellectual, creative, social, emotional, physical and spiritual nourishment, and how to be responsible for their own well-being in these areas, along with the importance of their civic responsibilities? It is my earnest contention that the excessive demand for much of the luxury, distraction and stimulation that cripples well-being in modern society would quickly attenuate if this knowledge and skillful self-care was developed early in life. And because part of the full-spectrum nourishment process is the identification of barriers and learning ways to overcome them, many of the challenges people usually end up facing much later in life would be addressed before they had layered years of self-destructive choices on top of each other. At least, empowered with such knowledge and skills, they could make truly informed choices about how to engage the world around them...and about how to more wisely consume various goods and services. In this way, much suffering would be relieved.

This brings us full circle to the main consideration, which is the *holistic value* of *perverse utility trade* in our proposed political economy. If such trade is no longer taboo, is no longer illegal, is no longer penalized, but instead placed in its appropriate place of *less desirable due to its poor nourishment quality* (i.e. an established, widely understood, low *holistic value*) then it can participate in a market without distorting that market or disrupting holistic nourishment. There will still be some addicts, compulsive gamblers, sexual predators and folks who seek to medicate anxiety or obsessive compulsive disorders with one *perverse utility trade* or other, but under the train-test-monitor model, they can be more rapidly identified, and offered appropriate help.

[To really push the envelope, we could extend this model still further, into territory that in many developed societies is highly conflicted within the rule of law: reproductive rights. It has already been observed by many researchers that once cultures around the world achieve a minimal level of economic stability, basic early education, and basic human rights for women, then birth rates begin to slow. By some estimates, this indicates the global population itself may begin to stabilize within the next few decades as world cultures continue to develop and women gain more education, equality and power. This is a great hope for me, since I believe a continuation of the human population explosion we have seen over the past century will quickly eviscerate planetary ecosystems and resources, along with any chance for long-term human survival. But if population stabilization really will occur this quickly, it still leaves us with an important question: who should have children? The presumption throughout much of human history has most often been that anyone who can reproduce is free to reproduce. I find this presumption astonishing. Instead, because of the sheer size of our projected population and its intense consumption of resources, I believe there should be some mechanisms for mitigating human reproduction.

As part of those controls, we could call upon the same train, test and monitor model. Folks who wanted to have a child could apply for a license, receive training, then test for child care knowledge, means and proficiency. Once they demonstrated at least a minimum level of competence, forethought and provisioning capacity, they could then receive a license for a child. Established metrics for child well-being could be used to assess successful parenting, and allow assistance to be offered to those who may be struggling. There could then be any number of additional mechanisms to determine how many children were allotted to a particular family, perhaps considered in a democratic way at the community level. It seems obvious that, where global population self-stabilizes or not, such an approach could be universally implemented.]

Why Market-Centric Capitalism is Unsustainable

Although arriving late in this discussion, *why* we need to be looking at alternatives to capitalism probably demands a brief overview. First, we should establish that capitalism, and in particular U.S.-style capitalism - what I have referred to as commercialist corporationism - is by far the most prevalent and powerful component of political economy in the world today. This has been true for roughly the past 150 years. Indeed alternatives have either collapsed, as in the case of the U.S.S.R., or for other reasons turned to market-centric practices, as in the case of China. So...why is this status quo a problem? Doesn't the dominance and success of commercialist corporationism for over a century prove its worth? Hasn't capitalism civilized and integrated the world through trade? Don't the benefits of capitalism far outweigh it's disadvantages? Well, actually no, none of this is completely true. Many folks have composed carefully detailed critiques of capitalism and its deleterious consequences. Some influential contemporary voices include Noam Chomsky, Naomi Klein, Greg Palast, Robert Greenwald, Joel Bakan, David Schweikart, Chris Hedges and Michael Moore, but there are many others. I have also written about the shortcomings of our particular flavor of capitalism in several essays and books. It is fairly straightforward to summarize the most negative impacts when nearly everything becomes *private* property available for trade; these include:

- The irreversible destruction of irreplaceable individual species and entire ecosystems on planet Earth. Among other equally tragic things, this results in a loss of biological diversity and interdependence that developed over billions of years, which in turn undermines the stability of Earth's biosphere as a whole, and of course the quality of human existence as well. Whether via pesticides and industrial pollution, or the unrelenting decimation of natural habitat for agriculture and housing, or industry-induced climate change, or the devastating damage wrought by wars over resources, or the reckless consumption of water and wild animals...privatization and trade have consistently led to widespread ecological destruction.

- The depletion of nonrenewable natural resources that not only have added much value to human civilization in the past, but could prove to be a dangerous deficit for future generations once they are fully depleted.

- An increasing homogenization and commoditization of culture that facilitates ubiquitous distribution of equally homogenous goods. This enables global economies of scale and a corresponding amplification of profit in everything from production and distribution to service and other secondary markets, but it also depletes humanity of a cultural diversity that has proven essential to human survival over time. The resulting intellectual, creative and cultural poverty-of-mind is in many ways just as threatening to our future survival as the depletion of nonrenewable natural resources.

- A deliberate conditioning of consumption habits that create lifelong dependencies and interrupt healthy self-nourishment. I have called this "externalization," which is simply the incorrect and disempowering assumption that all paths leading to physical, emotional, spiritual and intellectual nourishment (i.e. happiness, love, satiation, contentment, safety, success, belonging, purpose, etc.) are dependent on the consumption of goods and services provided by other people. This estrangement from the wealth of internal, self-sufficient resources available to every human being contributes to the povertization of individuals and cultures, and to an increasing number of health problems among commercialized populations. These include: chronic depression; obesity and Type II Diabetes; addictions to nicotine, alcohol, caffeine and various prescription drugs; ADHD and other childhood developmental deficits; anxiety and stress disorders; carpel tunnel syndrome; cancer; various patterns of compulsive, excessive consumption; and of course long dark nights of the soul. Many of these consequences are now considered epidemics in America.

- The exaggeration of hierarchical class divisions between people around the globe, where the lowest class, which is brutally and mercilessly exploited by all other classes, makes up ninety per cent or more of the population, and the most elevated classes, which receive ninety percent of the benefit of all production, make up less than ten percent of the population. Not only is this exploitation morally reprehensible, it also inevitably leads to deep antagonisms and conflict between the classes, which has already resulted in violent revolutions, ongoing terrorism and the intermittent threat of full scale war.

- The endangerment of all inhabitants of Earth through the constant striving of nation states to gain the upper economic hand using (or threatening to use) increasingly lethal and widely proliferated weapons of mass destruction.

- The demonstrated tendency for severe swings in economic stability as the result of excessive risk taking, deceptive efforts to manipulate trade mechanisms for greater profit, ignorance of externalities, monopolization, and of course the lack of regulatory controls to reign in such behaviors. These lead to inevitable market inefficiencies and failures.

- Extreme concentrations of wealth and influence in corporations, which in turn undermine democracy through cronyism. In the U.S., corporations write legislation that favors their industry and then fund the elections of politicians who vote that legislation into law. Corporations also aggressively fund political propaganda campaigns that misinform voters about legislation or politicians that do not favor corporate agendas. And, as a final blow to any hope of reversing these trends, corporations have also secured constitutional protections under a fiction of "corporate personhood," which they themselves legally engineered. These and other trends illustrate a continuous erosion of political, economic and democratic freedom and power - on a global scale - for all but a tiny minority of plutocrats.

- As a more subtle but pervasive consequence of U.S.-style capitalism, the constant growth and expansion pressures inherent to that system have created excessively rapid pacing in the development, production and distribution of new technologies. This has accelerated changes in human habits, interactions and society to such a degree that our ability to adapt vacillates between high levels of stress as we attempt to comply with change, to an irrational backlash of rejecting change because it is happening too fast. Neither of these polarities is constructive or supportive to human mental, emotional, physical or indeed spiritual faculties.

- In terms of moral creativity and function, market-centric capitalism inevitably constrains morality to its lowest common denominators. For example, acquisitiveness is preferable to generosity; deception is honored above honesty; hostile competition is rewarded more than cooperative kindness; callous disregard for others is valued more than compassion or empathy; and so on.

These outcomes are well-documented, longstanding and indisputable impacts of U.S.-style capitalism, and have manifested in almost every culture where this particular feudalistic memeplex has taken root. In addition, a perfect storm of destruction has manifested where three key influences intersect: first, growth-dependent capitalist economies drive accelerated innovation, production volume and resource utilization that far exceed the ability of individuals and society to adapt or the Earth's natural systems to sustain; second, the obsession with increased, short-term profits, combined with consumer addictions to newer, cheaper, sooner and more, have undermined quality, durability, reliability and safety in nearly all products and services to a devastating degree; and third, technological complexity is growing exponentially, far exceeding human capacities to manage interactions, predict outcomes or measure externalities.

It consistently astounds me that the advocates of commercialist corporationism so aggressively deny these destructive consequences - to the point where they spend hundreds of millions of dollars on disinformation campaigns, fabricated research and puppet scientists to maintain the status quo. Cigarettes don't cause cancer; global warming is a hoax; fracking is perfectly safe; pesticides are harmless; the Iraq war wasn't about oil; Teflon isn't dangerous; corn syrup is no different than cane sugar; American healthcare is the best in the world; red meat is part of a healthy diet; asbestos won't hurt you; nuclear power is "clean energy;" fast food doesn't cause obesity; greed is good for America; private education is always better than public education; deregulation is always good for consumers; ethanol is good for the environment; GMO crops are harmless; Oxycontin isn't addictive; and so on ad nauseum. The lies are endless, and are mainly intended to fortify power or profit, but they are effortlessly undermined with an overwhelming accumulation of contradictory facts...for anyone willing to search them out. And yet the desperate advocacy of a failing, toxic and highly destructive system marches on, often accepted without question by a naive and trusting public, a public has been carefully conditioned to conflate capitalism with personal freedoms, creature comforts, tribal identity and nationalistic pride.

My take on why this memeplex has expressed itself in these unfortunate ways is that U.S.-style capitalism has incorporated certain pernicious memes from the Western cultural tradition. Memes that are aggressive, dominating, violent, subjugating and destructive, but which have propagated Western culture around the globe, annihilating or subordinating anything in its path. I think the "coloniality of power" concept touches on these patterns in a meaningful way, and is well worth exploring (see Anibal Quijano, Maria Lugones, Walter Mignolo et al). In any case, almost all market-centric philosophies still embody these predatory memes. For our purposes, such memes illustrate that market-centric economies in their predominant form actually interfere with nourishment in several dimensions, disrupt moral development in favor of moral stagnation or regression, destroy moral creativity as we have defined it - confining moral vocabulary to a few base impulses - and do not by any stretch of the imagination operate with a guiding intentionality of transformative, all-encompassing love-consciousness. Yes, this form of capitalism has accomplished many constructive feats in record time, but it has increasingly become an outmoded means of exchange. It is time to move on.

Diagram: Contrasting Production Dynamics

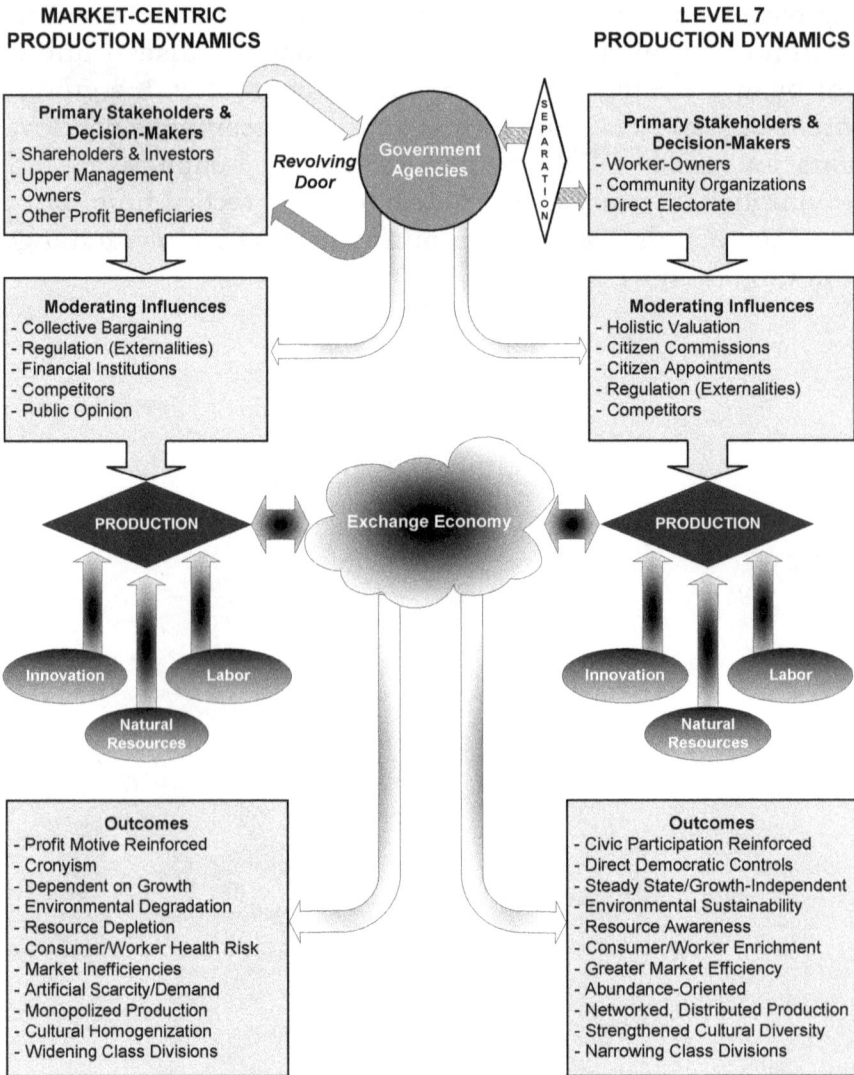

MARKET-CENTRIC PRODUCTION DYNAMICS

Primary Stakeholders & Decision-Makers
- Shareholders & Investors
- Upper Management
- Owners
- Other Profit Beneficiaries

Revolving Door

Government Agencies

SEPARATION

LEVEL 7 PRODUCTION DYNAMICS

Primary Stakeholders & Decision-Makers
- Worker-Owners
- Community Organizations
- Direct Electorate

Moderating Influences
- Collective Bargaining
- Regulation (Externalities)
- Financial Institutions
- Competitors
- Public Opinion

Moderating Influences
- Holistic Valuation
- Citizen Commissions
- Citizen Appointments
- Regulation (Externalities)
- Competitors

PRODUCTION

Exchange Economy

PRODUCTION

Innovation   Labor
Natural Resources

Innovation   Labor
Natural Resources

Outcomes
- Profit Motive Reinforced
- Cronyism
- Dependent on Growth
- Environmental Degradation
- Resource Depletion
- Consumer/Worker Health Risk
- Market Inefficiencies
- Artificial Scarcity/Demand
- Monopolized Production
- Cultural Homogenization
- Widening Class Divisions

Outcomes
- Civic Participation Reinforced
- Direct Democratic Controls
- Steady State/Growth-Independent
- Environmental Sustainability
- Resource Awareness
- Consumer/Worker Enrichment
- Greater Market Efficiency
- Abundance-Oriented
- Networked, Distributed Production
- Strengthened Cultural Diversity
- Narrowing Class Divisions

Next Steps?

So that is a my current take on why and how we should pursue a more morally advanced political economy - one that retains the best features of a mixed economy, distributed government and direct democracy, while more consciously expressing the *unitive principle*. I can't pretend to understand all the complexities that such a transition would involve, and yet I hold a profound conviction that this is both possible and necessary. The sentiment to do so is already present in the general populace, and can only continue to grow. Whether the entrenched elite recognize this inevitability and are willing to gracefully step out of the way or even aid in the transition is, however, a separate question. Some, I believe, have seen the writing on the wall, and are already willing to invest in a new way of being. Imagine the impact of billionaires helping fund community land trusts across the country, or voluntarily ceding control of their companies to a worker-cooperative model, then helping finance worker buyouts of other companies. But in terms of comprehensive change agency, I suspect several threads need to be engaged at the same time. First, a new vision needs to available to everyone, across all cultural and class divides, so that Level 7 memes can replicate.

To that end, this book can be downloaded under the Creative Commons Attribution-NonCommercial-ShareAlike 3.0 Unported License. ☐ In the same vein, since integral practice of multidimensional nourishment is such an important aspect in the training and cultivation of moral creativity, guidelines for this practice also need to be made freely available. You can find downloadable versions here: http://archive.org/search.php?query=t.collins%20logan.
To explore the theoretical framework of Integral Lifework, the book *True Love* is fairly meaty. *Being Well* is a more simplified introduction, and the end of the book has a description of Integral Coregroups designed to develop a community of support for integral practice, help promote multidimensional nourishment, then duplicate themselves.

These and other self-nourishment tools will help provide important foundations, but what of expansion into other arenas beyond the personal and interpersonal? What about community activism, democratic reforms and increased consumer awareness? As alluded to earlier, a plethora of organic and systemic change mechanisms are available to us, and we have touched upon how modeling new distributed, egalitarian and communal processes is a necessary element of this evolution. I also suspect traditional components like worker solidarity, civil disobedience and populist uprisings will also play an important role in the U.S. and elsewhere. Entrepreneurs who wish to champion the *unitive principle* can certainly add to the momentum by establishing worker-owned cooperatives and community organizations, and I've provided some resources at the end of the book that can assist in those efforts. At the same time, legislation could also be enacted that facilitates worker-buyouts of established businesses and implementations of direct democracy at community, regional and national levels.

Once again, I firmly believe that the desired outcomes of revolution and evolution should be expressed in their implementation, for we cannot expect a more loving world to arise from hate and violence. As Ralph W. Sockman famously said, "Be careful that victories do not carry the seed of future defeats." To that end, I recommend reviewing Gene Sharp's work on nonviolent revolutions at www.aeinstein.org. Paulo Freire's classic *Pedagogy of the Oppressed* is also a worthwhile read regarding the implementation of educational models and methods, and also in the broader context of communal dialogue and mutual liberation across class lines.

Beyond this, I also suspect activism and anarchism in the uppermost OSI layers will play a crucial role, in the form of free and open information that challenges the status quo, such as WikiLeaks, and a disruption of the modi operandi of the most recalcitrant, destructive and oppressive elements of commercialist corporationism. In particular, socially engaged art can have a significant impact not only in raising awareness around certain issues, but also engaging community in participatory solutions (Nato Thompson has documented many such efforts). I believe mass media of all kinds is a critical target for such actions, in order to change the message on a sufficient scale. Hactivists such as the group Anonymous can also make an important contribution, though I think they would do well to integrate a broader base of citizen action and support.

Instigating the constitutional reforms necessary for more top-down restructuring will require the slow, inexorable momentum of a large political movement. Right now, although some of the seeds have been planted through the Occupy and TEA Party efforts, the existing political establishment is too stuck and resistant for those seeds to grow. However, in combination with the other approaches described here, perhaps some cracks will form in the recalcitrant shell of state and national legislatures, allowing the light of liberty and reason to shine through. In fact, recent popular initiatives in Colorado (Amendment 65) and

Montana (I-166) indicate such cracks may indeed already be underway.   For more information about meaningful constitutional reform, check out the resources at www.reclaimdemocracy.org, www.movetoamend.org, and www.theallliancefordemocracy.org.

All of this advocacy and disruption is necessary to, as Aristotle might say, achieve the equitable above and beyond the just, and to help revitalize participation in civil society. As such, they are acts of *agape*; love-consciousness in action. All of these elements have been developing for some time, but the breadth of popular support - and the reach and intensity of evolutionary action - that are necessary to effect major change have yet to be sustained.   For an ultimate success defined by humanity and the Earth's mutual thriving, a Level 7 political economy would need to deploy globally and be championed by the planet's leading producers and consumers, while at the same time cultivated and modeled in the developing world.   Why? Because asymmetries in moral development will tend to undermine unitive implementations.   There are ways to navigate imbalances, and Shann Turnbull's elaborations on ownership transfer corporations (OTCs) and producer-consumer cooperatives (PCCs) may be helpful here.   But isolated pilots that cannot replicate themselves are insufficient.   So again we return to the drum beat of widespread grass roots activism coinciding with widespread top-down institutional change, both harmonized with the *unitive principle* so that enduring fruition can occur.

All of this can be made more spontaneously available through an increasingly advanced and more intimately shared moral creativity around the globe.   In a way, activism should reflect the multidimensional nourishment itself, so that purposeful action occurs in all twelve dimensions.   There will be intellectual debate, artistic expression, physical expression, evolution in the quality of our closest relationships and the consciousness of our sexuality, new forms of supportive community and spiritual practice, integrity with our core values and sense of purpose in how we relate and consume, and, above all, a unifying love-consciousness that embraces and energizes all dimensions. To whatever degree these supportive structures are in place, the possible becomes the probable.

Undoubtedly, our greatest challenge will be to shun the complacency plaguing the U.S. in this age of dependent consumption; we must end the society of the spectacle and embrace civic responsibility, increasing our self-awareness and self-sufficiency. "Therefore," as Aristotle wrote, "if there is an end for all that we do, this will be the good achievable by action..." and further, as a warning, "But most people do not do these, but take refuge in theory and think they are being philosophers and will become good in this way, behaving somewhat like patients who listen attentively to their doctors, but do none of the things they are ordered to do. As the latter will not be made well in body by such a course of treatment, the former will not be made well in soul by such a course of philosophy." Throughout the intervening centuries, these truths still hold.

To conclude, as we consider how to best address the challenges of modern democracy, Aristotle's own final words in his *Nicomachean Ethics* are potent and relevant reminder of one way to proceed:

> "First, then, if anything has been said well in detail by earlier thinkers, let us try to review it; then in the light of the constitutions we have collected let us study what sorts of influence preserve and destroy states, and what sorts preserve or destroy the particular kinds of constitution, and to what causes it is due that some are well and others ill administered. When these have been studied we shall perhaps be more likely to see with a comprehensive view, which constitution is best, and how each must be ordered, and what laws and customs it must use, if it is to be at its best. Let us make a beginning of our discussion."

Table: Fulfillment Impulses

FULFILLMENT IMPULSE	ACTIVE EXPRESSION	FELT SENSE
Discovery	Observe/Explore/Expand/Experiment	Sense of adventure, risk, opportunity
Understanding	Contextualize/Evaluate/Identify/Interpret	Sense of purpose, meaning, context, structure
Effectiveness	Impact/Shape/Actuate/Realize	Sense of activity, success, achievement, accomplishment
Perpetuation	Stabilize/Maintain/Secure/Contain	Sense of safety, family, security, "home"
Reproduction	Sexualize/Gratify/Stimulate/Attract	Sense of attraction, arousal, satisfaction, release, pleasure
Maturation	Nurture/Support/Grow/Thrive	Sense of caring, supporting, growing, maturing
Fulfillment	Complete/Transform/Transcend/Become	Sense of wonder, awe, fulfillment, transcendence, self-transformation
Sustenance	Taste/Consume/Quench/Savor	Sense of fullness, enjoyment, contentment, satiation
Avoidance	Escape/Evade/Deny/Reject	Sense of fearfulness, self-protectiveness, wariness, stubbornness
Union	Accept/Embrace/Incorporate/Combine	Sense of "being," union, interdependence, continuity
Autonomy	Differentiate/Individuate/Rebel/Isolate	Sense of distinct self, uniqueness, freedom, personal potential
Belonging	Cooperate/Conform/Commit/Submit	Sense of belonging, trust, community, acceptance
Affirmation	Appreciate/Enjoy/Celebrate/Create	Sense of "I am," play, gratitude, aesthetics, inspiration
Mastery	Empower/Compete/Dominate/Destroy	Sense of strength, power, control, skill, competence
Imagination	Hypothesize/Consider/Extrapolate/Project	Sense of limitlessness, possibility, inventiveness, "aha"
Exchange	Communicate/Engage/Share/Interact	Sense of connection, intimacy, sharing, expression

Additional Resources

After Capitalism (New Critical Theory), David Schweickart, 2011, ISBN 978-0742564985

Europe's Promise: Why the European Way Is the Best Hope in an Insecure Age, Steven Hill, 2010, ISBN 978-0520261372

The ABCs of Political Economy, Robin Hahnel, 2004, ISBN 978-0691003849

Building Sustainable Communities: Tools and Concepts for Self-Reliant Economic Change, C. George Benello, Shann Turnbull & Ward Morehouse, 1997, ISBN 978-0942850369

Building Powerful Community Organizations, Michael Jacoby Brown, 2007, ISBN-13: 978-0977151806

Democracy at Work: A Cure for Capitalism, Richard D. Wolff, 2012, ISBN 978-1608462476

The Cooperative Workplace: Potentials and Dilemmas of Organizational Democracy and Participation, Joyce Rothschild & Allen Whitt, 1989, ISBN 978-0521379427

Putting Democracy to Work: A Practical Guide for Starting Worker-Owned Businesses, Frank T Adams, Gene Taback & Gary B Hansen, 1993, ISBN 978-1881052098

For All the People: Uncovering the Hidden History of Cooperation, Cooperative Movements, and Communalism in America, John Curl, 2012, ISBN 978-1604865820

What Then Must We Do?, Gar Alperovitz, 2013, ISBN 978-1603585040

Living as Form: Socially Engaged Art from 1991-2011, Nato Thompson (Editor), 2012, ISBN 978-0262017343

Women's Education in Developing Countries, 1993, Elizabeth M. King & M. Anne Hill, ISBN 9780801845345

www.ingramcontent.com/pod-product-compliance
Lightning Source LLC
Chambersburg PA
CBHW031318040426
42443CB00005B/126